Cicero and the
Catilinarian Conspiracy

Routledge Studies in Ancient History

Cicero and the
Catilinarian Conspiracy

Charles Matson Odahl

Routledge
Taylor & Francis Group
New York London

First published 2010
by Routledge
270 Madison Avenue, New York, NY 10016

Simultaneously published in the UK
by Routledge
2 Park Square, Milton Park, Abingdon, Oxon OX14 4RN

Routledge is an imprint of the Taylor & Francis Group, an informa business

© 2010 Taylor & Francis

Typeset in Sabon by IBT Global.

Library of Congress Cataloging-in-Publication Data
Odahl, Charles M. (Charles Matson), 1944–
  Cicero and the Catilinarian conspiracy / by Charles Matson Odahl.
    p. cm. — (Routledge studies in ancient history ; 1)
  "Simultaneously published in the UK—T.p. verso.
  Includes bibliographical references and index.
  1. Rome—History—Conspiracy of Catiline, 65–62 B.C. 2. Rome—History—Conspiracy of Catiline, 65–62 B.C.—Sources. 3. Cicero, Marcus Tullius. 4. Catiline, ca. 108–62 B.C. 5. Cicero, Marcus Tullius—Political and social views. 6. Catiline, ca. 108–62 B.C.—Political and social views. 7. Catiline, ca. 108–62 B.C.—Influence. 8. Rome—Politics and government—265–30 B.C. I. Title.
  DG259.O33 2010
  937'.05—dc22
  2009042843

ISBN10: (hbk) 0-415-87472-6

ISBN13: (hbk) 978-0-415-87472-4

Dedicated to
My Special Muse
Penelopeia

Contents

Preface

When I was a young boy growing up in California, I used to love visiting my grandfather's study, which had one wall lined with oak wood and glass door bookshelves that were seven feet high and another wall displaying historical artifacts. Among the books in the former was a sixty-volume set entitled *The World's Greatest Literature*. One of the books which caught my eyes was subtitled "The Orations of Cicero." As I read through Cicero's speeches— specifically the *Orations against Catiline*—I was impressed with the brilliant eloquence of the man and with the dramatic danger of his times. I got to learn much more about Cicero and to study his works in Latin during my BA and MA degree programs in Ancient History and Classical Languages through the California State University system. While working at Yosemite National Park in the summers between my graduate studies, I enjoyed reading his *Orationes in Catilinam* in their ancient Latin versions and studying widely in the scholarship of the Roman Republic in my spare time. I took three years off from advanced university degree work to travel and study abroad, visiting archaeological sites and museum collections, and designing and leading study tours across Europe and the Mediterranean. As the job market for professorial positions in Classics was narrowing in the 1970s when I entered the doctoral program at the University of California, San Diego, I continued my studies in Greek and Roman History as minor fields, but stretched into Medieval History and Patristic Literature as my major fields. The latter emphasis in my Ph.D. degree program from UCSD has led to a research and writing career focused upon Constantine and Christianity with many publications in that field, including my recent wide-selling *Constantine and the Christian Empire*. While much enjoying the travel, research, speaking, and writing related to the latter field, I have never forsaken my early love for Ancient History and Classical Latin. Fortunately, my longtime university position at Boise State University with a two-year teaching cycle has allowed me to devote alternate years to three Ancient History and Classical Latin courses and to three Church History and Patristic Latin classes. In the former I have been able to keep up my interest and expand my knowledge of Roman History and Ciceronian Latin—particularly in my history seminar on Cicero and the Late Republic and in my Latin seminar on the

Ciceronian Age. Thus, after some thirty years of teaching about Cicero and the Roman Republic in American and European universities and leading tours to Ciceronian sites in Italy, I have written this book, *Cicero and the Catilinarian Conspiracy.* I have tried to do for Cicero and Catiline in this new work what I did for Constantine and Christianity in my earlier tome, i.e., offer a readable, up-to-date, and definitive account of an important episode in Roman history, which may prove interesting to ancient history students and to educated general readers alike.

What follows is a detailed historical narrative of the rise and fall of the Catilinarian Conspiracy in the decade of the 60s BC. It is set within and offers a case study of the political, military, economic, and social crises of the late republic during what has been called the "Roman Revolution." It chronicles the efforts of the defeated radical politician Lucius Sergius Catilina to bring together a group of disaffected Roman nobles and discontented Italian farmers in a conspiracy to overthrow the republican government at Rome and to take control of the Italian peninsula while the proconsul Pompey the Great and the majority of Roman military units were campaigning in the Near East, and the success of the conservative optimate consul Marcus Tullius Cicero in uncovering the conspiracy, driving Catiline out of Rome, and defeating his revolutionary followers in the capital and in Etruria. The narrative reveals the political corruption, economic problems, and military instability that were leading to the demise of the republican system and the rise of an imperial government in the first century BC. Some reflections on the similarities of the problems in the late Roman Republic to the divisive politics in many modern states are offered at the end of the last chapter.

I have shielded the narrative from the hyper-critical analysis of texts employed by some recent classicists, which results in achingly boring prose, and from the politically correct ideology in academia preferred by some modern historians, which leads to morally neutral language. In regard to the former, it has been argued on the basis of contradictions in the sources that the Pisonian or "First Catilinarian Conspiracy" did not occur and should be left out of the story. Unfortunately for those within this school of thought, rumors about this "conspiracy" circulated widely in the late 60s, were used in political and court speeches, were reported in the ancient sources, and undoubtedly influenced peoples' actions toward Catiline. It therefore must be included in the narrative (albeit as a rumor) and the debates about it among scholars confined to the endnotes so as not to harm the narrative flow. In regard to the latter, the spreading of scandalous rumors and the uttering of vicious invectives against one's opponents ("the politics of personal destruction," to use a modern phrase) were regular parts of late republican politics and cannot be ignored, and the employment of purple adjectives was a common practice among ancient authors and cannot be avoided. Although many of the negative charges and scurrilous language used in Roman political campaigns and in ancient historical sources may not have been true, the lack of such terminology in the historical narrative to please modern sensitivities is unrealistic. And on the basis of their provable actions, some ancient politicians were less morally upright than others and did not hesitate to employ open violence against their enemies. Thus, dismissing these elements from this story would make an objective and accurate presentation of the Ciceronian Era impossible. Such will not be done herein.

As this work is aimed at both ancient history students and educated general readers, any necessary Latin terms are explained in the book, scholarly debates are reserved for the endnotes, and a lucid style of writing has hopefully been employed throughout the text. Relevant maps and illustrations through the work take readers to the places where events in the story occurred; and a reasonable set of notes and bibliographic listings at the end allow curious readers to pursue further study in the ancient sources and modern scholarship upon which this book about Cicero and the Catilinarian Conspiracy is based.

I would like to thank the many people who have helped to make the research and writing of this book a pleasant experience: my professorial mentors Drs. Elemer Nagy and Loy Bilderback at Fresno State University, and Drs. Alden Mosshammer and Stanley Chodorow at the University of California, San Diego for training me in ancient history and classical languages; my Department Chair Dr. Nicholas Miller and colleagues at Boise State University, who have supported my teaching and writing career for three decades; the thousands of students in my history and Latin classes who have inspired my teaching and writing; the staffs of the Columbus Hotel in Rome and the Villa Aurora in Fiesole, who have made my many sojourns with them for research at Ciceronian sites in Rome and at Catilinarian sites in Tuscany most delightful; Humberto DeLuigi and Marta Fodor at Art Resource in New York for providing museum prints for four illustrations, and John Kelly and Carrie Quinney at the Simplot-Micron Instructional Technology Center in Boise for converting eight of my slides for the other illustrations in the book; my diligent graduate students Kasey Reed and Karen Wadley at BSU for proofing the typescript, and my dear professional colleagues Dr. Hans Pohlsander of SUNY Albany in New York, Dr. Mark Smith of the College of Idaho in Caldwell, Idaho, and Professor Joseph Kurth at Treasure Valley Community College in Ontario, Oregon (and some sagacious anonymous readers for Routledge) for reading drafts of the typescript of this book and making valuable suggestions for improving the text of the work; and Laura Stearns, Commissioning Editor, and Nicholas Mendoza, Editorial Assistant for Classics at Routledge/ Taylor & Francis Group, and Eleanor Chan of Integrated Book Technology in New York for seeing this book to publication.

Charles Matson Odahl
Villa Aurora in Fiesole

Illustrations

Chronology

I   The Subject and the Ancient Sources

"O what times, O what morals!"
Cicero, *Oratio in Catilinam* I. 1

In the dead of night they came together, moving stealthily from their various abodes to a private meeting at the house of a fellow conspirator deep in the center of ancient Rome. Here they wished to conceal themselves and their designs behind the secrecy of closed doors; for though their number included some of the higher officials and noblest names of the Roman state, the purpose of their gathering could hardly be considered commendable. They had not been summoned to indulge in one of the pleasant orgies for which they had become famous, but rather to receive the final instructions for their parts in a plot to seize control of the Roman Republic. To this conspiracy they had pledged their loyalty by an oath which was rumored to have been sealed with the drinking of human blood mixed with wine.

When all had arrived, the leader of this secretive coterie—a man of renowned passion, noted for the vigor of his physical prowess and the force of his emotional eloquence—solemnly began to address them. Referring to the failure of their earlier plans, he rebuked them for the torpid and timorous quality of their recent efforts, pointing out the great disdain and penalties they would suffer if detected as compared to the great power and wealth they would obtain if successful. He reported that the armed bands which had been raised throughout Italy were almost ready for action, and that he desired to leave the city as soon as possible to take command of the main force northward in Etruria.

Having raised their spirits and roused their courage with vigorous incitements to action, he laid out the final plans for their dangerous conspiracy. He designated those whom he would take north to join his army in Etruria, and those whom he would leave behind to direct the sedition in Rome. He explained that it would be the task of this latter group to assassinate the magistrates, to massacre a number of citizens, and to start fires throughout the city. As Rome would then be engulfed in confusion and conflagration, he would hastily march toward it with the revolutionary armies from the country districts in order to take control by force and stamp out any resistance which might be encountered. Yet, he lamented that there was one important matter which was delaying his departure—the fact that the consul who had been obstructing their designs was still alive and vigilantly following their every move. Two of his audacious followers volunteered to free him from this care and promised that they would slay the vexatious magistrate at dawn. When all understood their assignments and comprehended the gravity of the situation, the meeting broke up with each sanguine for the success of their daring venture.

This meeting occurred on the night of 6 November 63 BC at the home of a Roman senator of the distinguished Porcian clan. He and many of the men present that evening were of noble lineage and had held or were then holding magisterial positions in the Roman government. Several had reached the office of praetor, one even that of consul. They had been summoned to this secret nocturnal gathering by another noble of patrician lineage, Lucius Sergius Catilina. He was the originator and driving force behind this conspiracy to overthrow the Roman state and seize control of the Italian peninsula. The consul who stood in his way and whom he wished to slay was the eloquent orator and distinguished statesman Marcus Tullius Cicero. The actions of the latter would ultimately foil the designs and defeat the forces of the former. However, the clash of these two men and the political coalitions they championed electrified Rome during the decade of the 60s, and it was representative of the increasingly violent and chaotic nature of political life during the last decades of the late Roman Republic.[1]

When encountering this dramatic episode in Roman history, one cannot help but ask the following questions: What were the political and economic conditions which nourished such a destructive design? What manner of man was Catiline, and why was he motivated to undertake his perilous plot? What kind of leader was Cicero, and how was he able to build a political coalition to defeat Catiline? What were the relationships of Catiline and Cicero with the other famous men of the era, such as Pompey, Crassus, Caesar, and Cato? And finally, what was the effect of the Catilinarian Conspiracy upon the course of late republican history, and does this episode have any relevance to modern republics?

For answers to these questions, scholars of Roman history must turn to the ancient sources which provided information about the conspiracy of Catiline and the career of Cicero. There were two contemporary authors in the late republic who recorded the most detailed accounts of the clashes of Catiline and Cicero and several later authors from the early empire who offered narrative histories of the era or biographies of leading figures therein.

Marcus Tullius Cicero, the optimate consul who defeated Catiline, wrote several works relevant to the episode—which prove the old adage that "the victors write history." Cicero's senatorial orations, public addresses, court speeches, and correspondence provided an intimate picture of the political, social, and economic conditions of the late republic and vividly delineated the leading figures of that turbulent age. Very important among this literary corpus were his *Orationes in Catilinam* (*Orations Against Catiline*), four speeches given in senatorial meetings or before public audiences which detailed his charges against Catiline, the nature of the conspiracy, the manner in which he obtained evidence against the conspirators, and what he felt should be the penalties against them.

Although these orations have immortalized his adversary as the epitome of the vicious revolutionary, one can find among his later speeches and private letters a more objective portrayal of Catiline's character—an appraisal not colored by the immediate promptings of personal fear and political enmity. Gaius Sallustius Crispus, a *popularis* politician and analytical historian, was the other contemporary author who has left works relevant to the revolutionary events of the late republic. He had been a young man preparing for political life during Cicero's consulship, and he went on to serve in lower magisterial positions in the 50s and as a field general and provincial governor supporting Julius Caesar in the latter's civil wars and dictatorship in the 40s. The assassination of his patron in 44 BC turned him away from political activities and to historical writing over the next decade. The greater part of his *Historiae* (*Histories*), a narrative of the dozen years prior to the conflicts of Cicero and Catiline (78–67 BC), has mostly perished. Yet, in his two remaining extant monographs on the *Bellum Iugurthinum* (*The Jugurthine War*)—an account of a provincial war in late second century North Africa, and the *Bellum Catilinae* (*The War of Catiline*)—an account of the Catilinarian Conspiracy in mid-first century Italy, Sallust offered case studies of the dangerous politics and the leading players in the revolutionary era of the late republic. While giving Cicero his due for foiling the conspiracy in the latter work, he was more concerned with telling the story of Catiline and his followers and detailing the motives for their dangerous plot. The pro-popular and analytical works of Sallust have served to balance the evidence against the pro-optimate and self-congratulatory writings of Cicero. The strengths and weaknesses of these two literary giants, in fact, complemented each other: Cicero was precise in regard to chronology while Sallust was not; Sallust, on the other hand, recorded vital details which Cicero was not at liberty to divulge in his public addresses, e.g., the names and activities of Cicero's agents and informers during the conspiratorial machinations; and although Sallust was in basic agreement with Cicero in condemning the conspirators, he did so in a somewhat more detached manner, and thus offered a more well-rounded portrait of the people ensnared in the political clashes of the era.

Related in subject matter to the contemporary works of Cicero and Sallust listed above was the *Enarratio ad Orationem in Toga Candida* (*A Commentary on the Oration in the White Toga*) by Quintus Asconius Pedianus—a commentary on the famous election address which Cicero delivered against Catiline during the heated consular campaign of 64 BC. Asconius was a Roman grammarian and historian of the early empire a century after the Ciceronian Era, but he had immense interest in and considerable knowledge of late republican politics and personalities. As this ancient oration of Cicero does not survive independently, Asconius performed a vital service for modern historians by quoting from and commenting upon portions of it and by preserving the information which was contained within it about the early career of Catiline and the opinion of Cicero about his adversary.

Four narrative histories covering the late republic were written during early imperial times: two in Latin—those of Velleius Paterculus and Annius Florus; and two in Greek—those of Appianus and Cassius Dio Cocceianus. Velleius lived at the beginning of the imperial period and was a distinguished soldier and military commander under the first two emperors Augustus and Tiberius. In his later years he wrote a cursory history of the republic entitled *Libri Duo Historiae Romanae (Two Books of Roman History)*. Its basic weakness was its brevity, especially with regard to the conspiracy of Catiline. Yet, Velleius did present some useful background information in a fairly objective manner, and his biographical sketches of the leading protagonists of the Ciceronian Era were skillfully drawn. Florus was a contemporary of the emperor Hadrian a century later, and wrote a two book *Epitomae de Tito Livio Bellorum Omnium Annorum DCC (An Epitome of All the Wars of Seven Hundred Years from Titus Livius)*—a summary of the wars of the Roman people from the founding of the city down to the end of the republic as told in the massive 142-book history of the Augustan author Livy. As the books of the latter on the late republic have not survived, Florus gave some idea of what had been in them. Although the *Epitomae* suffered from superficial brevity and rhetorical excess, it did contain a chapter on the "War of Catiline" that offered a dramatic narration of many important details from the later stages of the conspiracy. Appian was a native of Egypt who, after obtaining Roman citizenship, became a civil servant in Rome during the mid-second century. He was fascinated with the glories of Roman imperialism, and he devoted his later years to writing a substantial series of histories dealing with Roman warfare. The *Bella Mithridatica (Mithridatic Wars)* and the *Bella Civilia (Civil Wars)* were the ones from his corpus relevant to this study—the former with respect to the military career of Pompey and the latter in regard to the internal struggles of the late republic. In the *Bella Civilia*, Appian devoted a substantial section to the conspiracy of Catiline and offered many details about it. There were some key omissions in the work (e.g., Catiline's defeat in the consular election of 63 BC) and some inaccuracies in chronology, but it offered more useful information than the two Latin narratives. Dio, a high and trusted official of the Severan emperors in the early third century, was the farthest removed in point of time from the Ciceronian Era. Yet he spent some twenty years researching and writing a massive *Historia Romana (Roman History)* from Rome's beginnings down to AD 229, and the result of his effort was an invaluable source for modern historians. Of the extant narrative histories, that of Dio (even with some anti-Ciceronian bias) ranked above the others in correct chronology, in extent of detail, and in accurate presentation of the facts.

Two ancient biographers have left literary portraits of some of the leading political figures of the late republic—Gaius Suetonius Tranquillus in

Latin and Plutarch in Greek. Suetonius served as a secretary to the emperor Hadrian in the early second century and was able to consult official sources when writing his *De Vita Caesarum* (*On the Life of the Caesars*). Only the first biography in this work, *Divus Julius* (*Julius Caesar*), is relevant to this book. It provided data on the early career of Caesar and his political alignments and intrigues during his rise to power in the decade of the 60s. One has to be careful in using it, however, for Suetonius had a tendency to give Caesar more credit than he deserved during those early years. Plutarch, an older contemporary of Suetonius, was a Greco-Roman scholar who read extensively and traveled widely in Greece and Italy, was honored by the emperors Trajan and Hadrian, and ended his days in literary productions and priestly activities at the shrine of Apollo in Delphi, Greece. Known as the "prince of ancient biographers," he left an extensive corpus of forty-six *Bioi* (*Lives*) of Greek and Roman statesmen and generals. Among these were the *Lives* of important late republican leaders, such as the Gracchi brothers, Marius, Sulla, Pompey, Crassus, Cicero, Cato the Younger, and Caesar, which filled up numerous gaps in the extant historical narratives. Plutarch admittedly had his faults—an overemphasis on the supernatural, a passion for anecdotes, and at times an uncritical analysis of his sources—but these were certainly outweighed by the vivid portraits and vast volume of information he has left modern historians on the outstanding individuals of the ancient Roman world.

Besides these ancient literary sources, there are some geographic sites and some material remains that can assist scholars in imagining the physical environment in which the clashes of Cicero and Catiline occurred. The *Forum Romanum* (Roman Forum) in the heart of modern Rome still exhibits the site of the assembly ground, a Senate House, and temple ruins in and/or around which much of the political action in this story took place; the hills of Tuscany around modern Florence display the remnants of the ancient town of Faesulae (modern Fiesole) where Catiline mustered the major force of his revolutionary armies and the mountain pass at Pistoria (modern Pistoia) where he died in defeat.

After detailed analyses of the ancient sources and extensive reading in the modern scholarship relevant to the topics under scrutiny herein, I have attempted to construct an historical narrative which answers the questions raised by the Catilinarian Conspiracy. The account centers on the careers of Catiline and Cicero—one directed the rise of the conspiracy, the other its fall.[2]

II The Late Republican Setting

"Now the institution of parties and factions with all their attendant evils originated at Rome."

Sallust, *Bellum Iugurthinum* 41. 1

During the early republic (509–264 BC), the Romans had evolved a classic "check and balance" republican system of government that consisted of annually elected magistrates headed by consuls who directed executive matters at home and military campaigns abroad, a permanent aristocratic Senate which oversaw public finances and foreign affairs, and assemblies of the people which elected magistrates and enacted legislation. They had also established an efficient military made up of citizen militias known as legions and organized in flexible lines and centuriate groups of foot soldiers. In this period Rome had conquered the peoples of Italy and unified them in a confederation of cities that adopted republican governments and sent auxiliary soldiers to the legions. During the mid republic (264–133 BC), the Romans had become an imperial power by conquering Carthage in the west and setting up provinces in Sicily, southern Gaul, Hispania, and North Africa and by defeating the Hellenistic kingdoms in the east and establishing provinces or client kingdoms through Greece, Asia Minor, the Near East, and Egypt. The Greek statesman and historian Polybius thought that the stability of the republican system and the flexibility of the legionary armies were key elements of Rome's success in becoming the dominant imperial power and the most prosperous state across the Mediterranean by the middle of the second century. The political and military successes of these early periods had come with minimal internal strife and had led to rises in the material well-being of the Roman people and in the cultural achievements of Roman civilization.

However, the conquest of a vast Mediterranean empire caused profound changes in the political, economic, and social aspects of Roman culture. These changes brought about a series of political crises that wreaked havoc with the republican constitutional framework and eventually resulted in its demise. The period of troubles that occurred during the late republic (133–31 BC) began with the revolutionary actions of the Tiberius and Gaius Gracchus to initiate land reforms in the late second century and ended with the military triumphs of Julius and Augustus Caesar to establish imperial rule in the late first century. This hundred-year period of recurring civil conflicts has often been called the era of the "Roman Revolution," and the Catilinarian Conspiracy was one of the revolutionary episodes within and representative of it.[1]

Looking back over this period from the last decade of the late republic, Sallust thought that he could locate the change for the worse in Roman political culture a little after Rome's defeat of Carthage for control of the western Mediterranean Basin (146). He felt that before then the Romans had been forced to be united against a powerful common enemy and had been accustomed to put public concerns above private goals in a virtuous defense of their state. He believed that afterwards they were able to march easily over all enemies and revel luxuriously in the spoils of an enlarging empire without the dread of a rival power. Fear of the enemy had preserved the good morals of the commonwealth:

> Yet when the minds of the people were relieved of that dread, wantonness and arrogance—the vices of prosperity—naturally arose. Thus, the peace for which they had longed in times of adversity proved to be more cruel and bitter after they had gained it than adversity itself. For the nobles began to abuse their position and the people their liberty, and each man robbed, pillaged, and plundered in his own interest. Thereafter the republic was split into two parties, and between these the state was torn to pieces. The nobles were the more powerful faction as the strength of the commons was incompact and divided among many. Affairs at home and wars abroad were managed according to the will of a few men, in whose hands were the treasury, the provinces, the magistracies, glory and triumphs. The people were burdened with military service and poverty while the commanders divided the spoils of war with a few friends. Meanwhile, the parents or the children of the common soldiers, if they had a powerful neighbor, were driven from their homes. Thus, with the acquisition of power, unlimited and unrestrained greed arose, and it violated and devastated everything, holding nothing sacred and bringing about its own downfall. Yet, when nobles were found who preferred true glory to unjust power, the state began to be disturbed, and civil dissension arose like an upheaval from the earth.

In this manner, the historian Sallust described the beginnings of the political crisis of the republic in his *Bellum Iugurthinum*. In another pithy passage in the *Bellum Catilinae*, he commented that "first the lust for money, and then the desire for power arose; such things as these were the roots of all evils." Sallust was a moralist at heart and perceived the root cause of the republic's problems as a failure of the Romans to uphold the *mos maiorum*, the "customs of the ancestors," the pristine morals by which earlier generations had made Rome a great power.[2]

Although Sallust had a tendency to glorify the virtues of earlier generations in comparison to his own, he did hit the mark in many areas of his appraisal of the late republican setting. Before the history of this chaotic period in general and the clashes of Cicero and Catiline in particular can be understood, a description of the political climate of the late republic must be offered. In view of the fact that much of the action in this story centered upon the Roman Senate, the members, factions, and policies of that body need to be outlined. Because the conspiracy touched all elements of Roman society, the position of the equestrians, of the yeoman farmers, and of the landless urban mob in the political framework of the time should be surveyed. And as the menacing shadow of the contemporary military hero Gnaeus Pompeius had no small effect upon the actions of Roman politicians during the Ciceronian Era, the entrance of the military into politics during the late republic must also be considered.

The Roman Senate had long been the central governing agency of the Roman world. It was the only continuous consultative body within the republican constitutional framework and thus, of necessity, had directed the acquisition of Rome's empire. The magistrates of the state and many of the jurors for the courts were chosen from among its members. It had oversight of public finances and controlled assignments to military and provincial commands, and it was considered the governing power at Rome by foreigners.

The Senate was the nerve center of Roman political life in Cicero's day; but the *patres conscripti* (the "conscript fathers" as the senators were sometimes called) were then beset with internal strife. Since the late second century, the Senate had often split into factions or coalitions with their adherents seeking political supremacy at the expense of their adversaries. Cicero offered a somewhat biased definition of these factions when he said:

> There have always been two kinds of men in this state who have sought to engage in public affairs and to distinguish themselves therein. Of these two kinds, one aimed at being, by repute and in reality, *populares*, the other *optimates*. Those who wished everything that they said to be agreeable to the masses were reckoned as *populares*, but those who acted so as to win by their policy the approval of the best citizens were judged as *optimates*.[3]

These ancient factions were certainly not political parties in the modern sense of the term "party." They did not have regular party organizations with permanent central committees, official financial organs and publicity machines, or formal tickets on election ballots. They were simply political alliances and social groupings of men from the noble and senatorial ranks who held different views on constitutional matters and public policy and employed different methods to attain their common objective: political dominance in the Roman Republic.[4]

The *optimates* were an influential circle of wealthy landowners who had long held majority control of the Senate and styled themselves as the *boni* ("the good men"), whose duty it was to uphold the traditional position of the Senate as the chief governing body of the state. They often united their families together in *amicitia*—bonds of "friendship" and intermarriage for the purpose of supporting the electoral campaigns and policy initiatives of their leading members. Through the use of the patron–client relationship they contrived to control the annual election of the higher magistrates in the *Comitia Centuriata* (the Assembly of Centuries) in such a way that the consulships and praetorships would most often fall to themselves; and they clearly regarded the consulship as their own "to pass . . . on from one to another of their number." In this manner they were able to reserve for themselves the lion's share of the spoils of empire. Sallust commented on this when he had Catiline say: "It is always to them that foreign kings and potentates are tributary and peoples and tribes pay taxes. . . . Thus all influence, power, office, and wealth are in their hands or wherever they wish to bestow them."[5]

The leaders of the optimate faction in the Ciceronian Era included Quintus Lutatius Catulus, a consul in 78, who had crushed the anti-senatorial Lepidan revolt; Lucius Licinius Lucullus, a consul in 74, and the commander in the early stages of the third war against Mithridates; Quintus Caecilius Metellus Creticus, a consul in 69, and the conqueror of the island of Crete; Quintus Hortensius, the other consul in 69, and a renowned orator and leading advocate in the Roman courts; and Marcus Porcius Cato, elected tribune for 62, who emerged from the Catilinarian episode as an important spokesman of the optimate cause. Their goals were essentially conservative: to protect the public treasury and private property, and to maintain control over the governance of Rome and its empire. Many of them sincerely believed that the best interests of the republic and its subjects could be served by their control of the Roman government. Cato served as an excellent example of one of the better kinds of optimates as he was constantly insisting upon the duties and obligations of the Roman state to its subjects and allies. Yet many others were largely unconcerned for the welfare of the provincials, or even, for that matter, of the poorer classes of Roman citizens. The plundering of Sicily by its senatorial governor Gaius Verres presented an example of one of the worse kinds of optimate politicians.

The *populares*—though often of the same wealthy background as the *optimates*—were a smaller group in the Senate, who found themselves at odds with the majority on policy issues and hindered in their attempts to gain distinction by obtaining high offices. They styled themselves as the "proponents of the people's rights" and sent tribunes to the *Comitia Tributa* (the Tribal Assembly) without customary senatorial backing for bills submitted to the legislative assembly; there they procured enactment of laws favorable to the common people. As the spoils of empire were at stake, they did not want to sit back passively and watch the *optimates* line their purses while all that was left for themselves were "danger, defeat, prosecutions, and poverty."[6] Thus, they took advantage of the unsettled social conditions of the time to achieve their goals. By offering "reforms" to the oppressed lower classes of Roman society, they sought to attain popularity among the mass of the voting public to gain the support they needed to get elected to the offices and to get appointed to the commands which they desired.

Leaders of the popular faction in the Ciceronian Era included Gaius Aurelius Cotta, who had campaigned in the 70s for the restoration of tribunicial powers after they had been curtailed by the dictator Sulla; Marcus Licinius Crassus, the main conqueror of Spartacus, who as consul in 70 had supported the restoration of the pre-Sullan legislative powers to the tribunate; Gnaeus Pompeius Magnus, who as consul with Crassus in 70 had also backed the restoration of the tribunes' powers and then, by receiving extraordinary proconsular commands from the Tribal Assembly, had become the idol of the masses through his military exploits across the Mediterranean Basin; Lucius Sergius Catilina, who like Crassus and Pompey had begun his career as an optimate but later switched to the popular cause, and took control of the radical wing of the *populares* by offering lavish promises to the urban and rural poor in campaigns for the consulship in the mid 60s; and Gaius Julius Caesar, a nephew of the popular general Marius through his aunt Julia, who as aedile of 65 won great popularity with the urban mob by presenting lavish gladiatorial shows at festival games. The initiatives that they often sponsored were usually liberal measures, such as subsidized grain for the landless urban proletariat, land redistribution to dispossessed yeoman farmers, citizenship to unfranchised Italian allies, and debt reduction to debtors of all classes—all of which were opposed to the interests of the *optimates*. Although there seem to have been genuine reformers among the *populares*—particularly their founding father Tiberius Gracchus, who had been concerned about the declining position of the yeoman farmers in second century Italy—many of them were more concerned with gaining personal power than with alleviating the problems of the landless city mob, the debt-ridden farmers, and the oppressed allied and subject peoples of Italy and the provinces.

As could be expected, the *optimates* "strove with the highest effort . . . against these men, ostensibly in behalf of the Senate, but in reality for their own enhancement."[7] Since there were ten tribunes at this time, the *optimates* could usually get one or more of their supporters elected to this office and could oppose the programs of the *populares* with the latter's own methods, such as the use of the tribunician veto power, or through the introduction of legislative measures favorable to their cause in the Tribal Assembly. The *optimates* also had usually controlled most of the priesthoods of the state religion and could utilize sacred superstitions and old rites to delay or obstruct passage of the popular bills of their opponents. Sallust remarked that the intense struggles for power between these opposing factions in the Senate were carried out under "specious pretexts, some maintaining that they were defending the rights of the commons, others that they were upholding the prestige of the Senate; but, under the pretense of the public welfare, each in reality was working for its own advancement."[8] Or as an astute modern commentator on senatorial politics in the late republican era has stated: "the *optimates* were working for the maintenance of an oligarchy while the great figures who adopted popular methods were usually attempting to establish personal supremacy."[9]

Competition

In this contentious political climate, a decline in the morality among some of the governing class gradually occurred. Since only two consulships and ten praetorships were available each year, the struggle for these prestigious offices within a Senate of several hundred members was necessarily fierce and expensive. Therefore, bribery and violence were not uncommon occurrences during republican electoral campaigns. Among many of the nobility, luxury and extravagant display were the fashion while prestige and political position were the goals. A nineteenth-century historian described the political game thus:

> Vast wealth was to be found among the nobility, but also vast indebtedness; for politics was an expensive pursuit, and no man could hope to succeed who was not as lavish in flinging away his money as he was unscrupulous in getting it. A young man spent all he could borrow in forcing his way to office . . ., for office would be a certain mine of wealth. When his consulship or praetorship had expired he was assigned a province and then he made his harvest.[10]

But to obtain office—and the power and wealth which came with it—members of the senatorial factions had to secure electoral support from the other elements of the Roman citizen body. Thus, the positions of the equestrians, the yeoman farmers, and the urban mob within late republican society must be surveyed.

While the senatorial order comprised the landholding aristocracy of Rome, the *equites* were the moneyed class. As the senators were forbidden by law to engage in business, it was the equestrians who handled the business activities necessary for the governance of a great world empire—banking, tax farming, road constructions, etc. The *equites* were usually men from the upper- and middle-class Roman and Italian families who had chosen to forego the rigors of the political arena and to make their fortunes instead through business activities. A young *eques*, destined for a senatorial career by his father's wishes, expressed the equestrian aversion to politics when he recorded in his autobiography:

> I received the first honors of young manhood, and was once a part of a three-man city commission. Yet, I left the *curia* behind and had the purple stripes on my shoulder drawn in; politics was too great a burden for my powers. My body was neither enduring enough, nor my mind suitable for such labor; therefore, I avoided the anxious campaigning for office. . . .[11]

Nevertheless, a career in politics was always open to young men of equestrian background who preferred "the anxious campaigning for office" to the the traditional business pursuits of their family. These men could expect to serve in some of the lower magisterial positions of the republic, such as quaestorships (finance officers and military quartermasters) and aedileships (public works officials and religious festival organizers) and earn a seat in the Senate; but to gain the consulship, Rome's highest office, was a different matter. Only the most talented could hope to attain that closely guarded pinnacle of power. Marius, through extraordinary military exploits in the late second century, and Cicero, through outstanding legal and oratorical skills in the mid-first century, were among the select group of equestrians who made it into the top ranks of the senatorial *nobiles*.

As men of business, the *equites* were inclined to support whichever senatorial faction or program was most beneficial to their business interests. For instance, when a popular politician offered a bill to an assembly of the people that would give Pompey an extraordinary military command, the equestrians would support the measure in spite of optimate opposition because Pompey would probably conquer new territory and establish new provinces, which would further their money-lending and tax-farming activities. On the other hand, if a popular leader were to promise a program of debt cancellation, the equestrians would quickly join ranks with the optimate faction in defense of property rights. Generally, the *equites* were likely to take the side of the conservative *optimates*, who were for the maintenance of the status quo, rather than that of the liberal *populares*, whose schemes might endanger the financial position of the equestrians. Although "there was no love lost between the business men and the governing class . . ., upon the whole there was a tacit understanding between the two classes to divide the spoil."[12]

The backbone of Roman society had long been the small independent farmers of the Italian countryside. Since the end of the Second Punic War (218–01 BC), they had been a diminishing breed—the hapless victims of imperial expansion and a changing economy. While the conquest of an overseas empire had brought great wealth, increasing luxury, and escape from the toils of the field to the senatorial and equestrian classes, the yeoman farmers had been burdened with long military campaigns, new economic competition, and mounting debts.

Much of the land which Rome had conquered from her Italian neighbors during the early republic had been added to the *ager publicus populi Romani* (the public land of the Roman people) and used for the foundation of colonial towns loyal to Rome and for the establishment of farms leased to Roman citizens. Wealthy nobles of the senatorial class had often taken over control of these public lands and combined them with their ancestral holdings to create large estates known as *latifundia*.[13] With the acquisition of the provinces of Sicily and North Africa and the influx of grain tribute from them in the mid republic, the cereal grains produced by the small independent farmers of central Italy were no longer essential to the economy of Rome. Thus, the large landowners had shifted to stock raising and vine and olive cultivation, and had brought in slave labor to work their estates. Unfortunately, very few peasant farmers had either the monetary resources or the agrarian knowledge necessary to make the changeover from grain growing for domestic consumption to other forms of production for the international market; nor were they able to compete successfully with the cheap labor and efficiency of the *latifundia*. When they were called away on military campaigns for long periods of time, their lands might be out of cultivation when they returned, or even worse, "if they happened to have a powerful neighbor, their parents or young children might well have been driven from their homes." They had to borrow money to get started again and often then went into debt, "and a series of bad years placed them at the mercy of creditors anxious to acquire land."[14] If they could not meet their financial obligations, it was relatively easy for the creditors to seize their land as the common people were exposed to the full rigor of the Roman laws of debt much more than the powerful men who could fight back. The plight of these farmers can be gleaned through the words which Sallust imputed to Gaius Manlius, one of Catiline's leading rural followers in Etruria:

> We are wretched and destitute, and many of us have been driven from our country by the violence and cruelty of the moneylenders, while all have lost reputation and fortune. None of us has been allowed, in accordance with the tradition of our ancestors, to enjoy the protection of the law and to retain our personal liberty after being stripped of our patrimony—such was the inhumanity of the moneylenders and the praetor.[15]

The founding fathers of the popular movement, Tiberius and his brother Gaius Gracchus, had attempted to limit the size of the senatorial *latifundia*, to confiscate excess land from them, and to redistribute these parcels in order to reestablish small peasant farms in the late second century; but they had been assassinated by agents of the optimate oligarchy for the revolutionary methods they had used to do so. Some progress had been made in parts of Italy (occasionally even with senatorial backing) in land redistribution programs through the early first century. Yet, as the comments of Manlius above demonstrate, the problems of displaced and debtor farmers still festered in the 60s, and distressed areas in the peninsula served as fertile beds where the seeds of discontent could be planted by radical leaders.

The land problem in the Italian countryside, in turn, was increasing the instability of the political climate in Rome. For many discouraged and debtor farmers who had sold or lost their rural land were moving to Rome; and as landless poor, they congregated in the capital to eek out a living as day laborers, to become the political clients of senators, and to enjoy the exciting allurements of the big city instead of the thankless toil on the farms. Cicero related that the *capite censi* ("those counted by the head," the landless urban mob) were recruited by the nobles of both senatorial factions to be their political clients. In return for an apartment or an allowance and the promises of inexpensive grain and exciting games, these landless citizens would give their political loyalty and votes to a senatorial patron. They would come to greet him at his home in the morning and follow him through the streets to the assemblies or Senate House to make him look important, and they would cast their votes for him or his political allies for the higher offices of state in the *Comitia Centuriata* or for the legislation he supported in the *Comitia Tributa*. The leading political *nobiles* of the late second and first century thus had gangs of clients in Rome who acted as their informal bodyguards, guaranteed voting blocks, and street thugs willing to use violence on their behalf. This situation boded ill for the continuing viability of republican institutions since the urban mob did not represent the Roman citizen body as a whole, yet it could provide a large number of votes needed to pass legislation in the *Comitia Tributa* binding upon all citizens. Sallust reported that it was among the urban mob that the *populares* leaders primarily sought their support, for "if a man is ambitious for power, he can have no better supporters than the poor; they are not concerned about their own possessions since they have none, and whatever will put something into their pockets is right and proper in their eyes." The popular leaders offered programs that would win them a large following among the urban mob, and then were able to secure the passage of measures which they needed to increase their personal power—especially extraordinary military commands.[16]

It was the rise of the politician-generals and the entrance of the military into active political participation which was the most dangerous aspect of the late republican setting. At about the time when Cicero and Catiline were born in the last decade of the second century, the *popularis* leader Gaius Marius, by appealing to the Tribal Assembly, had been given supreme command of the war in North Africa against the Numidian king Jugurtha, superseding the senatorial appointment Quintus Caecilius Metellus Numidicus. Although this in itself was contrary to the long-established custom of senatorial control over foreign affairs, his subsequent action was even more revolutionary as Sallust later reported:

> He himself meanwhile enrolled soldiers, not according to the citizen classes in the manner of our ancestors, but by allowing anyone to volunteer, for the most part the *capite censi*. Some say that he did this through lack of good men, others out of a desire to curry favor since that class had given him honor and rank.[17]

Marius probably had been motivated by both of the suggested reasons, but undoubtedly the lack of Roman citizens eligible for military service had been his immediate concern. This situation had come about because of the decline of the small peasant farmers, the backbone of the Roman legions. The traditional method of conscripting only landholding citizens was no longer working when that class was declining and Rome had a great empire to defend. So, Marius had done the logical thing and allowed members of the landless city mob to enroll in the Roman legions. In doing so, he had been able to redeem the prestige of Roman arms by finally defeating the elusive Jurgutha in North Africa (107–104 BC), and by thoroughly conquering the German *Cimbri* and *Teutones* in southern Gaul and north Italy (102–101 BC). However, by the enlistment of the *capite censi*, Marius had brought the military into politics—a dangerous situation in any commonwealth. The legionaries became the dependents of their general. They looked to him for a career and booty when under his command and for support and land when they retired: "and after they were established in colonies with grants of land they continued to regard him as their patron, to look to him for aid, and to respond to his call in time of need."[18] In essence, the general had become the patron of his soldiers, and the soldiers had become the clients of their general in political affairs.

The three great politician-generals during the lifetime of Catiline were Gaius Marius, under whose shadow Catiline entered the world and grew to manhood; Lucius Cornelius Sulla, under whom he entered upon a public career; and Gnaeus Pompeius Magnus, his renowned contemporary and a probable obstacle to his designs for power. Each of these men had significant influence not only upon the careers of Catiline and Cicero, but also upon the unstable atmosphere of late republican politics. Marius and Sulla provided examples for Pompey, Crassus, Catiline, and Caesar that an important consideration when attempting to attain supreme power in the republic should be the support of loyal and dependent armies. Marius had used his soldiers and the urban poor to get elected to seven consulships at the head of the popular faction in the late second and early first centuries (107, 104–100, and 86 BC). Sulla had marched his loyal troops against Rome twice in the decade of the 80s—first to retain the assignment of a great proconsular command against the eastern king Mithridates, and then to take control of Rome for the optimate faction by force, kill off most of his political opponents, and become dictator for three years (87–79 BC). There was some political stability under optimate rule in Rome in the following decade; but the careers of Marius and Sulla had left a residue of fear in all politicians—*optimates* and *populares* alike—of the possibility of further civil wars and of murderous proscriptions if a powerful general should again be able to march on the capital and destroy his rivals. And Sulla had further intensified the land problem by uprooting many yeoman farmers in Italy to provide land grants for his veterans. In fact Etruria, the area most severely affected by these confiscations, was to provide a very fruitful recruiting ground for Catiline's agents in the 60s.

Although the influence of the military was becoming a dominant factor in politics, the political conflicts of the time were still waged within the framework of the optimate and popular factions of the senatorial nobility. Both Marius and Sulla had been senators, and each had headed the interests of an opposing faction—Marius the *populares* and Sulla the *optimates*. Pompey, however, confused the situation somewhat by fighting first under the banner of one faction and then the other, thus raising himself to a position of unprecedented glory and power at the expense of both. Catiline was to follow the same procedure, but with entirely different results.

Pompey had begun his career as a supporter of Sulla, raising an army to help the optimate commander overcome the popular forces holding Italy and Rome in the late 80s. During the next decade, he had become the "golden boy" of the Senate, receiving from it a series of commands to crush revolts of popular leaders (Lepidus in Italy, Sertorius and Perperna in Spain, and a remnant of the Spartacan slave army in Etruria—the majority of which had already been defeated in southern Italy by his political rival Marcus Crassus). Yet, the impressive string of victories by Pompey in extraordinary commands had soon begun to worry the senatorial oligarchy—*numquam eminentia invidia carent* ("the eminent are never without envy").[19] They withdrew their support from him, and turned to others of their number for important imperial commands (Lucius Lucullus against a resurgent Mithridates in Anatolia, and Quintus Metellus against pirates on Crete). To the consternation of the optimate faction, Pompey switched his allegiance and, along with Crassus, ran as a *popularis* candidate for the consulship of 70 and won. By sponsoring or allowing the enactment of a number of popular measures while consul (supporting the restoration of the power of tribunes to initiate legislation and the reinstatement of the equestrians to some positions in Roman courts), he undermined optimate control of the government. Pompey was soon rewarded by popular tribunes and the Tribal Assembly with more of the extraordinary commands he coveted—against pirates across the Mediterranean in 67 and against Mithridates in the Near East in 66, which conferred upon him wider powers than any Roman general had ever possessed. He swiftly defeated the pirates and destroyed their bases in two lightning sea campaigns lasting only a few months each in the western and eastern Mediterranean; and then he proceeded to Asia Minor where he replaced the previous commanders Lucullus and Glabrio to bring the long wars against Mithridates to a final conclusion. Pompey would remain in the East for four years (66–62 BC). He was already the most powerful and most famous general in the history of the republic. In the next few years, he would greatly augment his reputation by a series of brilliant victories and marvelous exploits in distant and little-known lands on the borders of civilization which would see him compared to Alexander the Great of Greek history, and which virtually placed the eastern half of the Roman world under his patronage.[20]

The fear of what Pompey the Great might do when he returned hovered like a dark cloud over the minds of optimate and popular politicians alike and guided their actions during these years. For Pompey had not attached himself firmly to either of the senatorial factions. In fact, he had used both to gain his own goal of principal status in the republic. Thus, the senatorial *optimates* feared that upon his return he might set himself up as a dictator, carry out proscriptions, and strike the death blow to senatorial control of the republic. He also appeared to be a threat to *populares* leaders such as Crassus, Catiline, and Caesar, who wanted to attain position and power for themselves, but would be prevented from doing so if the notoriously jealous Pompey decided upon one-man rule. Therefore, the *optimates* wanted to hold on to and increase, if possible, what political power they still had; and the *populares* wished to strengthen their own positions and build up independent bases of power before Pompey returned from the East. Such was the political setting in the Roman world when Lucius Catiline conspired to overthrow the republican government and Marcus Cicero succeeded in defending it.

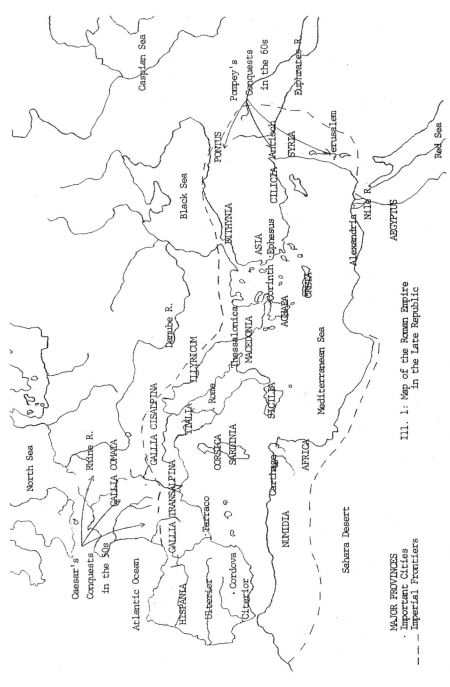

Ill. 1: Map of the Roman Empire
in the Late Republic

MAJOR PROVINCES
· Important Cities
— — Imperial Frontiers

Illustration 1 Map of the Roman Empire in the Late Republic.

III Catiline and the Radical Politicians

"Catiline was a person of note by reason of his great
celebrity and by high birth, but he was a madman."

Appian, *Bella Civilia* II. 1. 2

Late in the year 66, shortly after Pompey had departed for his extraordinary proconsular command in the East, Lucius Sergius Catilina returned to
Rome, having finished a propraetorian governorship in North Africa and
intent upon raising himself to Rome's highest magistracy. He found the city
engulfed in political strife. The controversy centered on the very office he
wished to obtain—the consulship.[1] Now that Pompey was off on campaign
and the popular faction was without a charismatic leader, the *optimates*
were attempting to reassert their control over the government. The summer elections had given mixed results to the oligarchy as men with popular
sympathies had won several important posts: Crassus had gained one of
the two censorships, Caesar an aedileship, and Publius Autronius Paetus
had secured one of the consulships (although Publius Cornelius Sulla, a
nephew of the former dictator, had been elected to the other one). However,
the *optimates* had struck back by employing the newly enacted Calpurnian
Law against electoral bribery to void the results of the consular election.
Autronius and Sulla had been convicted of bribery and stripped of their
offices. The stage was set for a second consular election in which the *optimates* expected to be victorious.[2]

Into this situation strode Catiline, and seeing the opportunity to obtain
the goal of most senatorial politicians, he immediately announced his candidacy. Catiline had been born into an old and noble patrician family, but
the fortunes of the Sergius clan had fallen to a low estate by the time of his
birth. In an era of extravagant display and widespread corruption, poverty
was an unbearable situation to a man of Catiline's ambition. So, he had
become a zealous adherent of Sulla and had collected all of the booty he
could from the victims of the dictator's proscriptions—apparently, enough
to carry him through the next decade. He had progressed through the
lower offices of the *cursus honorum* (the prescribed "course of offices"
for Roman politicians) in regular order and without marked distinction,
attaining the praetorship in 68. He then had spent the following year as the
propraetorian governor of Africa, fleecing the provincials in an effort to fill
his purse, which was rumored to have been drained by extravagant living
and electoral bribery.[3]

During these years it had not been Catiline's ordinary political career, but rather his checkered private life that had attracted the most attention. He probably was not one of the more virtuous members of his generation, but whether he actually committed all of the pernicious deeds which were attributed to him in contemporary sources is a matter of historical conjecture. It was alleged by Cicero and other ancient authors that among his bloody actions during the Sullan proscription Catiline had killed his own brother, and then he had persuaded Sulla to put the dead man's name on the list of the proscribed to make his fratricide appear legal. He was rumored to have had sexual relations with a virgin priestess of Vesta, to have deflowered a daughter, and to have been on terms of criminal intimacy with young men. Another rumor that was current in the 60s was that he had murdered his former spouse and son in order to clear the way for a union with his current beautiful but disreputable wife Aurelia Orestilla. However, not everyone knew of these rumors, and many who did probably felt that it was best to ignore them; for many of Rome's prominent citizens had been guilty of excesses during the Sullan Era. It was well known, for instance, that Crassus, Rome's chief financier and censor-elect, had become wealthy by preying upon the misfortunes of the proscribed, and that Pompey, Rome's great general and commander in the eastern war against Mithridates, had been too hasty in butchering some of the Marian popular leaders. Moreover, illicit relationships were common in the permissive and cosmopolitan society of Catiline's Rome, and his own new wife was certainly not as infamous as a lovely member of the noble Clodian family was soon to become.[4]

Catiline must have felt that his chances for election were rather good. He most certainly was qualified for the office. He had a noble pedigree, was a member of the Senate, and had served at home and abroad in all of the requisite positions leading up to the consulship. He possessed many attractive personal attributes. He was endowed with great strength both of body and mind and was renowned for his ability to endure hunger, cold, and lack of sleep. He was a man of great sensitivity and passion and was daring and versatile. He was well known for his generosity, loyalty, and devotion to friends, and his friends were numbered among all classes of society. His adaptable nature had allowed him to ingratiate himself with many diverse people, and he possessed the eloquence to be fully convincing to those whose support he might seek. Cicero later described him as a man who was able

> to guide and rule his natural disposition as occasion required, and to bend and turn it this way and that; to be serious with the austere, lighthearted with the lax, grave with the old, amicable with the young, daring with criminals, and dissolute with the depraved.[5]

Catiline was thus an ideal politician, a man who offered something to everyone. Yet his bright hopes were soon crushed by developments that he might well have expected: His candidacy was rejected by the officiating consul, and he was indicted for extortion.

As mentioned above, the family of Catiline was as poor as it was noble; and thus, monetary resources—and the debts acquired through the lack thereof—were to plague him throughout his career. Catiline was an ambitious, prodigal, and luxury-loving man. To live in the style he desired and to obtain the offices he wanted cost a great deal. By the time he had reached the praetorship, "he had reduced himself to poverty in order to gratify his ambition."[6] So, when he had gone out to his provincial assignment in North Africa, he had attempted to extort from the provincials as much money as he could obtain. Extortion was not the monopoly of the impoverished only, for other well-to-do Roman politicians practiced it. Yet, they would usually have to face an extortion trial when they returned home to Italy. This was no great setback, however, for it was often easy to bribe the court with their provincial loot and still have enough left over to live in high style until they bribed their way into another office. Although this method of advancement was not employed by all Roman politicians, it was used by Catiline and some of his extravagant contemporaries.

When Catiline returned to Rome too late to announce his run for the consulship within the specified time before the election, and word came back from Africa that the provincial subjects there wished to have him indicted for extortion, the consul in charge of the elections refused to allow his candidacy. He was forced to accept the situation and console himself with the thought that he would most likely be able to bribe his way to an acquittal on the extortion charge, and be able to stand for the consulship later. Yet, to a man such as Catiline, this was a heavy blow. He was probably angry at his fellow nobles for rejecting his candidacy and for allowing the extortion plea at this time. His loyalty to the optimate cause may have been shaken by these events.[7]

The new election resulted in a victory for the *optimates* as their candidates Lucius Cotta and Lucius Torquatus were selected to replace the ousted Sulla and Autronius. The former acceded to the decision of the courts and resigned himself to giving up the office to which he had been elected. But Autronius and Catiline may not have been so amenable to disappointment. According to a contemporary rumor, these incidents stung them to the core and made them wish for revenge. An opportunity for the latter presented itself in the person of Gnaeus Piso, whom Sallust described as "a young noble . . . of the utmost recklessness, poor and given to intrigue, who was being goaded on by the need for funds and an evil character to overthrow the government." It is reported that Piso approached Autronius and Catiline in December of 66 with a dangerous design by which they might seize power at Rome and abroad. The possibility that Catiline agreed to assume a leading role in this dubious plot revealed for the first time that he was willing to employ violent and illegal methods in order to gain power—an ominous foreshadowing of the future.[8]

Their plan was apparently to murder the replacement consuls as the latter were being sworn into office. The deed was to take place atop the Capitoline Hill on the first of January 65. In the resulting confusion, Autronius and Catiline would seize the consular *fasces*, take control of the government, and decree that Piso be dispatched with an army to occupy the two provinces in Hispania (probably as a base of power against Pompey). Supposedly, the conspirators were to be backed in this revolutionary *coup d'etat* by sympathetic members of the nobility and their clients among the urban mob. A rumor about the plot seems to have leaked out, for it was postponed until the fifth of February. During the interval, the conspirators revised their plans from just an assassination of the consuls to a general massacre of all those senators whom they felt would be a hindrance to their designs. On the designated day, Catiline was to take a certain spot in front of the Senate House in the Forum and give a signal to the conspirators when their victims were at hand. But according to most accounts, Catiline was overly anxious and signaled before a sufficient number of the plotters and their supporters were in their appointed positions with the result that no one made a move and the whole affair came to naught. After two failures, the conspirators were wise enough to put aside their risky scheme before too many people became aware of it.[9]

This fiasco has usually been labeled the "First Catilinarian Conspiracy." Yet this title is obviously a misnomer since Piso seems to have been the leading spirit behind it, and he should receive the credit for it instead of his more renowned accomplice. Many modern scholars have doubted that it even occurred, but the repeated references to it in the ancient sources and the general instability of the political climate in Rome seem to indicate that something dangerous may have been afoot in early 65. If this failed plot had been planned, it was a significant portent for the more dangerous schemes to come from Catiline in the near future.[10]

Another year and a half would pass before Catiline could step into the center of the Roman political arena again. During this period, he was faced with court trials and a rising pile of debts while his activities were less important than those of Crassus and Caesar. With the departure of Pompey, the torch of the *populares* had fallen into the hands of Marcus Crassus. This great financier and former consul was Pompey's chief rival for power within the ranks of the popular faction, and he was intensely jealous of the power and prestige which the great general then held. This rivalry was of twenty years standing and had started back in the Sullan Era. In Sulla's march on Rome, Crassus had fought as bravely and successfully as had Pompey; but it was to the younger man that Sulla had accorded the most honor and even the cognomen of *magnus*, "the great." The *dignitas* of Crassus had suffered another blow at Pompey's hands during the revolt of the gladiators in the 70s. Crassus should have been the true hero of the conflict that had raged up and down Italy, since it was he who had inflicted the final crushing defeat upon the armies of Spartacus. Yet Pompey, when returning from his successful campaign against Sertorius in Spain, had intercepted and slain the last fugitives from the Spartacan forces. He then claimed credit in a public letter to the Senate for putting a final end to the revolt, thus demeaning the hard-fought and valorous victory of Crassus. The fact that the latter had been forced to solicit the support of Pompey in order to win the consulship of 70 had been a further blow to Crassus' pride and surely had increased his jealousy of Pompey's power and status.[11]

Now that Pompey was far off in the East, Crassus desired to bolster his own position to the subversion of his rival's. Thus, he did everything possible to gain popular support and establish bases of power for himself while the conquering general was away. One of the means of doing this was to employ his wealth and influence to bring needy but useful politicians under his obligation. The failure of the inept "Pisonian Conspiracy" presented an ideal opportunity for enacting this policy. Many of the senators neither knew about nor believed in the rumored plot; but apparently some of those who did were trying to have it investigated. Crassus knew that Piso was neither a personal friend nor a political ally of Pompey and that Autronius and Catiline might be useful tools. Therefore, he used his influence to have the affair smoothed over and covered up, indebting the hapless plotters to himself. He even persuaded the Senate to rid the city of the dangerous Piso by sending him off to Hispania Citerior (Closer Spain) in the west as governor where he might serve as "a safeguard against Pompey, whose power was then too formidable." This sounded reasonable to the *optimates* who feared Piso's rabble-rousing activities in the city and who felt that Pompey needed a check. Yet in reality, this move was Crassus' first step in his attempt to build up bases of power which he might be able to use as levers against Pompey when the latter returned; for he fully expected the grateful Piso to support him if a clash came.[12]

As Crassus had been elected to the important office of the censorship for 65, he swiftly attempted to employ that post for the strengthening of his position at the expense of Pompey—and at that of the *optimates* as well. Upon assuming office, he proposed two measures which were aimed at winning him strategic support at home and abroad: 1) the granting of full citizenship rights to the people living north of the Po River in the province of Gallia Cisalpina; and 2) the annexation of Egypt as a province by his ally in the aedileship, Julius Caesar. The first proposal probably was aimed at bringing the Gauls of northern Italy under his patronage and gaining popularity in a large area where recruits for legions could easily be gathered. The second proposal concerning Egypt was even more far-reaching. Crassus apparently hoped to undermine Pompey's support among the *equites* by offering Egypt as a new field for their money-making ventures and to offset his opponent's military superiority by stationing Caesar (who, it was generally believed, was financially indebted to Crassus) with an army on the southern flank of Pompey. If all of the schemes of Crassus had come to fruition, it is obvious that he would have been in an excellent position to confront Pompey as an equal on the latter's return from the East. He would have had popular support at Rome among the *equites* and the urban poor and military support abroad in strategic places around the empire (Spain, Gaul, and Egypt).[13]

However, all of his efforts came to naught as one by one his plans fell through. Apparently, the Spaniards were no more disposed to Piso's character and activities than the Senate since they slew the tempestuous Roman shortly after his arrival. It is possible that Pompey had a hand in his death since it was rumored that the murder of Piso had been arranged by Pompeian agents in Spain. So, Crassus' far western base of support fell first. Then, behind the vigorous leadership of Quintus Catulus, the *optimates* blocked the other measures of Crassus. Catulus, the powerful and respected former consul (78), was the associate of Crassus in the censorship and therefore was able to veto the proposal for Transpadane citizenship. Having reached a stalemate on this issue, both censors resigned their office without fulfilling any of their other duties. Catulus next led the oligarchic opposition in the Tribal Assembly against the proposed Egyptian annexation. He and his optimate colleagues certainly wanted to check the power of Pompey, but they wished to do so without erecting a rival claimant to supreme power, especially a wealthy and radical *popularis* like Crassus. The *optimates* were backed on this issue by the *equites* and their rising star Cicero, who remained loyal to the interests of Pompey. Therefore, a coalition of Rome's landed and moneyed aristocrats prevented the passage of the last and most important of Crassus' power-grabbing schemes. Crassus must have feared that it was too dangerous to continue his anti-Pompeian and anti-optimate actions in the open, since he withdrew from the limelight thereafter and took up the role of a behind-the-scenes kingmaker. He threw his financial resources behind bold, popular politicians in order to accomplish his designs indirectly.[14]

Julius Caesar and Lucius Catiline benefited most from the generosity of Crassus. Yet, the anti-optimate actions of the former and the profligate conduct of the latter soon began to arouse apprehension among Rome's conservative establishment. The position of Caesar among the *populares* was most comfortable during the mid 60s. He had been one of the few nobles to support the measure for Pompey's Eastern command, and by this he had earned the great general's friendship. Through his support for the Egyptian scheme of Crassus, he had also obtained the wealthy financier's friendship and, most importantly, his monetary support. As a nephew of the wife of Marius and a colorful *bon vivant*, he was gaining popularity among the urban mob. However, having only reached the office of aedile, he posed no threat to the eminence of Pompey or Crassus or to the ambitions of Catiline. Since he was still several years away from the consulship, he seems to have perceived that the best policy to follow during these years would be to strengthen his popularity with the urban populace, to undermine the position of his political enemies, the *optimates*, and to play a helpful role to the current leaders of the popular faction.[15]

In conformity with these objectives, Caesar made himself a great favorite among the urban poor by outdoing all his predecessors in the aedileship with the magnificent public entertainments he offered at the public festivals during the year 65. Gladiatorial combats, theatrical performances, and public banquets had never before been presented on such a lavish scale—320 pairs of gladiators fought in one spectacular event! In doing these things, Caesar incurred heavy debts, but he was able to count on aid from "Crassus, the richest of the Romans, who had need of Caesar's vigor and fire for his political campaign against Pompey." Being the heir of Marius and popular with the urban masses, Caesar was most useful to Crassus, especially in his public actions against the *optimates*. He retaliated against the oligarchy for defeating the Egyptian plan by "restoring the trophies commemorating the victories of Gaius Marius over Jugurtha and over the Cimbri and Teutones, which Sulla had long since demolished." This action was a direct attack upon optimate prestige, for Marius had been one of the greatest of the early *populares*, and his memory was revered by the common people. In the year following his aedileship (64), Caesar further attempted to humble the optimate faction by indicting some of them for the murders committed during the Sullan proscription. Serving as a *iudex quaestionis* (judge) at these trials, he oversaw the conviction of and brought to punishment several of the accused.[16]

Caesar's popular activities greatly disturbed the optimate leadership, and they took measures to oppose him. They sponsored and passed a bill "limiting the number of gladiators which anyone was allowed to keep in the city," thus checking the extravagance of his shows. Catulus publicly rebuked Caesar in the Senate for restoring the Marian trophies, but the populace had received this act so favorably that the oligarchy did not dare to remove them. During these years (66–64 BC), Caesar was in a position to do no more than nip at the heels of the optimate oligarchy; he was several years away from eligibility for the consulship. Furthermore, Pompey was far off in the East, and the open activities of Crassus had been stifled by the resurgent *optimates*.[17] However, there was one other emerging leader of the *populares* whose chances for an upcoming consulship were excellent.

Lucius Catiline had been born into an old patrician family and seemed destined to be a member of the senatorial nobility. He had begun his political career as a supporter of Sulla and the optimate oligarchy. Yet, his disappointment at being barred from running for the consulship in 66 had soured him toward his old senatorial allies, and his rumored participation in the "Pisonian Conspiracy" of early 65 had revealed his move toward more radical circles. Because he faced an extortion trial in 65, he was prevented from seeking the consulship for another year. During this period, his ambition for power grew ever more impatient, and he gathered support from many quarters. The powerful and the poor, men and women alike courted his favor. As a rising star among the *populares*, his home became a leading social spot and a favorite "watering hole" for both radical young politicians and the needy urban masses. The amusements, banquets, amours, and money he supplied to his widening circle of friends and followers became well known across the capital city. He numbered among his associates some of Rome's noblest men; yet, he was also gathering around himself many people of questionable virtue.[18]

Catiline was becoming the man of the hour, the man who seemed destined for the consulship. So, when his extortion trial came up in 65, he had little trouble in gaining an acquittal. The best men stepped forward to defend him. Even Lucius Torquatus, the consul whom it was rumored Catiline and his co-conspirators had planned to kill, came to his defense. Marcus Cicero, Rome's leading advocate, considered offering his services. Cicero was a *homo novus* ("new man") from the equestrian class who was also aiming at the consulship. He hoped to earn Catiline's favor so that the latter might canvass with him for the office and better his chances. Yet, Catiline did not use Cicero; he seemed to be so certain of victory that he did not feel that he needed the services of the *inquilinus* ("the lodger"). There was little doubt that Catiline had been guilty of extortion in his African province and that it cost him a good deal of money to obtain an acquittal. This expense and the mounting debts piling up from extravagant living and lavish outlays to his friends were reducing him to poverty. He had another year to go before he could stand for the consulship in the summer of 64, and he needed money to maintain his current lifestyle.[19]

This situation presented an ideal opportunity to Crassus. As mentioned above, Catiline was already indebted to the great financier for smoothing things over after the rumored Pisonian plot, and Crassus probably felt inclined to strengthen that indebtedness now with more substantial support. Having a bold, reckless, and radical politician like Catiline in his political circle might be most useful, for—as Sallust later commented—Crassus "was willing to see anyone's influence grow in opposition to the power of his rival [Pompey]," especially if that person was heavily under obligation to himself. Caesar, following his financial patron and recognizing that Catiline was on the threshold of power, also threw his backing behind the rising *popularis*. Catiline was thus able to continue in his prodigal ways while Crassus and Caesar attempted to bring him under their influence by bribing him with money and favors. During the proscription trials of 64, Caesar demonstrated his support by helping him obtain an acquittal, even though Catiline was certainly just as guilty as the rest of the accused Sullan henchmen.[20]

As the campaign of 64 neared, the prospects for the *populares* and their new standard-bearer appeared encouraging. But on the political horizon the star of Marcus Cicero was rising—and he would come into direct conflict with Catiline and his backers.

IV Cicero and the Conservative Coalition

"Marcus Cicero owed his elevation wholly to himself, . . . and was as distinguished in his life as he was great in genius."

Velleius, *Historiae Romanae* II. 34. 3

Marcus Tullius Cicero, Rome's golden-tongued orator and leading trial advocate, also intended to run for the consulship in the summer of 64 and was to emerge as the chief competitor of Catiline during the final stages of the campaign.[1] Cicero had actually considered seeking the favor of Catiline during the latter's extortion trial by offering his services as counsel. Yet, he had not served in that position, and it is uncertain whether Cicero had not tendered the offer or whether Catiline had rebuffed him. In either case, an enmity arose between them during the ensuing year, and it came out into the open in the summer consular campaign.

Cicero had been born into a family of equestrian stock in the central Italian town of Arpinum a little to the south of Rome, and thus lacked the patrician heritage and noble pedigree of Catiline. However, by the mid-60s he had risen to a position of respect and influence in the highest circles of Roman politics by his successful pleadings in court cases and by his upright behavior in public affairs. He had started his political career at about the same time as Catiline; but as he was neither a member of an old aristocratic family nor inclined to the military arts, he had felt that his best chance for advancement was through the law courts. There he could put to use the learned vocabulary and the oratorical eloquence which he had acquired as a young man while studying under the finest rhetoricians and legal experts of the day. He had chosen the correct field for his endeavors as the convincing oratory, pleasant jesting, and biting invective of his court speeches had made him one of the most popular advocates during the decade after Sulla. When he bested the renowned Hortensius in the infamous Verrine trial in 70, he became the most sought-after forensic orator in the Roman courts.[2]

During these years, Cicero was progressing gradually through the political offices of the *cursus honorum*, hoping ultimately to obtain the consulship and to raise the status of his family to the nobility. He served as a quaestor in Sicily in 75, as an aedile at Rome in 69, and as a praetor there in 66. While holding these positions he gained a reputation for fairness and integrity. He lived in a modest manner, was conscientious to friends, and associated with the outstanding *literati* of the day. His reputation and influence were growing throughout Italy, and many important men—Pompey among them—considered his friendship a valuable asset. In regard to his political sympathies, Cicero had early in his career garnered more fame as a supporter of the *populares* than of the *optimates*. In fact, he had first gained widespread public attention by defending a man under indictment in the Sullan Era—the trial of Roscius of Ameria. His subsequent prosecution of Verres, the horribly corrupt governor of Sicily, certainly had not endeared him to the senatorial oligarchy— especially since this trial resulted in the Senate losing majority control of the juries to the financial class (*equites*). Nor did he bolster his standing with the *optimates* by his eloquent support of the Manilian Law, which transferred the eastern Mithridatic command to the popular champion Pompey after the optimate commanders Lucullus and Glabrio had failed to bring the war to an end.[3]

Yet Cicero was far from being a radical *popularis*. On the contrary, he was by nature conservative and devoted to republican institutions as his later and famous tract *De Re Publica* was to prove. He had sought popular support on his journey up the *cursus honorum* because as a "new man" he could hardly expect the exclusive senatorial *nobiles* to back him. By endorsing Pompey, he hoped for electoral support from the general's veterans and followers among the Roman populace. These elements, together with his original base of support among his equestrian friends in the Italian towns, would make him a formidable candidate for high offices. As any ambitious Roman politician, Cicero had always had his sights set on the consulship. To gain this position, however, he knew that he would also need some backing from the optimate nobles who controlled the upper and more powerful voting classes in the Centuriate Assembly.[4] Therefore, he had always endeavored to leave the door open for support from the senatorial oligarchy by tempering the attacks which he made upon their interests. For instance, when he had advocated that Pompey be given the Mithridatic command, he had been careful to generously praise the abilities of Lucullus, the optimate general in the earlier phases of the eastern war. He had also made his services as legal counsel available to *optimates* because he hoped that his courtroom eloquence might compensate for his deficiency in noble progenitors. Cicero's strategy for running a successful consular campaign was apparently to build a coalition of support from among the more conservative elements of the Roman electorate: the *equites*, the Pompeian *populares*, and the senatorial *optimates*. He had risen from the ranks of the Italian *equites* and already had an extensive following among them. He deserved the backing of the Pompeian *populares* as he had been most helpful to them. The question was: Could he overcome the prejudice of the senatorial *optimates* against "new men" and obtain their commendation for his consular candidacy?[5]

Cicero's chances of achieving this adroit political feat rose in the spring of 64 as Catiline's activities, associates, and statements appeared ever more menacing to the optimate faction; and Cicero was quite willing to do his part in convincing the senatorial oligarchy of his opponent's perversity. Catiline certainly was not immune to criticism, for by optimate standards the quality of his associates and the nature of his activities had seemingly degenerated in the months prior to the election. He still numbered among his friends some of the better class of Roman citizens, but he was associating more often with those individuals for whom no other term but depraved seemed accurate. As Sallust reported, he seemed to attract and enjoy the company of "criminals and reprobates of every kind." Wantons, gluttons, gamesters, and profligates flocked to his side and cast off their cares in the extravagant parties he was providing. But this kind of life could only blunt his physical and mental powers, leading to careless statements and reckless actions. Cicero remarked that "he was exhausting in lust and wantonness the forces that make for industry and assist virtue." Catiline's profligate activities certainly could not be expected to inspire the senatorial oligarchs with confidence in his ability to handle the dignity and duties of a consulship. Nor could the reports about his statements on debt cancellation, proscription of the rich, and other harebrained ideas lead to enthusiastic support for his candidacy by Rome's conservative nobility.[6]

Catiline was becoming a *persona non grata* to many of the *optimates*, but he was so certain of victory from the support which he had that he was oblivious to the loss of optimate backing. By the time of the election, he was openly playing the role of a radical *popularis* and seeking support from the popular faction of Crassus, frustrated politicians like himself, and debtor farmers throughout Italy—especially the discontented veterans of Sulla in Etruria. He had for a running mate the only other strong contender in the race, Gaius Antonius, a disreputable politician from a famous family like himself, and he was quite confident of success. He undoubtedly looked with contempt upon the chances of the "new man," expecting that the oligarchy would reject him and split their votes between the four other weak but acceptable candidates: Publius Sulpicius Galba, Lucius Cassius Longinus, Quintus Cornificius, and Caius Licinius Sacerdos. This attitude, however, was a grave error because Cicero was a consummate campaigner, and his convincing tongue could be as malicious as it was eloquent.[7]

Cicero was a master of the art of the personal campaign, and he had been laying the foundations for his electoral support for many years. He had developed a great ability to remember salient facts about his many acquaintances. He had accustomed himself to recall the names of Rome's notable citizens, the quarter of the city in which they dwelt, the area of Italy where they owned country houses, and the circle of their personal friends and political allies. In his daily walks to the Forum, he always would be escorted both by important politicians and loyal clients whose presence with him was calculated to create an impression of prominence among the citizen body. He would affectionately greet as many men of every social group and voting class as he was able, inquiring about the joys and woes of each in an effort to make them feel that he considered them important. He hoped in this way to gain as many votes as possible among the populace of the city. As did other senators, Cicero owned several country houses or villas across Italy, and he often traveled throughout the peninsula to visit friends and to establish contacts with municipal leaders whose votes would be most helpful in the Centuriate Assembly elections. Titus Pomponius Atticus, one of Italy's wealthiest and most influential equestrians, was a friend and confidant of Cicero, and he could be counted upon to employ his influence with the Roman nobility and Pompey's followers on behalf of his friend's candidacy.[8]

Cicero's own influence among the equestrian and senatorial ranks was becoming ever stronger because of his position as Rome's leading advocate. He used his oratorical talents in the courts mainly for the defense of important politicians. In this manner, he gained many influential friends whose support was essential in a consular election. For the sake of an example, he actually confided to Atticus in a letter during the campaign that he had taken the case of a certain noble client rather than that of another because he thought that it would be more beneficial to his chances of election to do so. One modern historian of the late republican era has suggested that Cicero withdrew his offer to defend Catiline in the latter's extortion trial late in the year 65 because he had perceived that the senatorial oligarchs were becoming disillusioned with Catiline's profligate activities, and that association with him was no longer of much value in obtaining optimate backing. In any case, Cicero knew whose support he needed, and he did everything in his power to obtain it.[9]

Accordingly, even though Cicero was a *homo novus*, and the *optimates* had not allowed one of these to obtain the consulship in several decades, he must have seemed to be a much more agreeable candidate to them than the reckless noble Catiline who was singing the tune of the radical *populares*. The audacious actions and lavish bribery of Catiline and Antonius during the final weeks of the campaign were open and flagitious violations of the Calpurnian Law and seriously disquieted senatorial leaders. The latter attempted to strengthen the bribery law by initiating a legislative measure which would establish more severe penalties for electoral abuses. But a pawn of the popular faction, the tribune Quintus Mucius Orestinus, interceded with a veto and blocked the measure. This brazen act on the part of the radical *populares* set the stage for the most important incident of the campaign—truly the turning point of the election.[10]

As if the shameless veto of Mucius were not enough to convince the wavering *optimates* to desert the prodigal patrician, Cicero arose in the Senate fired with the intent to deliver a slashing invective which would do so—his famous *Oratio in Toga Candida*. In essence, this "Oration in the White Toga" (the garment worn by candidates for office) was a fierce attack upon the spotted public career of Catiline and a biting exposé of his scandalous private life. Cicero vividly painted a sanguinary picture of a young Catiline viciously slitting the throats of the helpless victims of the Sullan proscription and then triumphantly toting their severed and bloody skulls through the streets of Rome. He upbraided him for harassing and despoiling the African provincials and then profaning and belittling the Roman courts with an acquittal gained through bribery. He reported the rumor that Catiline, along with Piso and others, had planned to slaughter the senatorial *optimates* in order to seize power for themselves a year and a half earlier. Turning to his private life, Cicero accused Catiline of violating the sacred halls of the Vestal Virgins, of committing adultery, and of living in an incestuous relationship with his own daughter. He vigorously portrayed Catiline as a paragon of violence and evil whose very presence in the consulship would contaminate the dignity of that office.

Cicero inveighed not only against Catiline, but also against his other detractors as well. He censured Antonius for despoiling the Greek provincials during his governorship in the east, for squandering his patrimony, and for being ungrateful to himself for aid in a former election. He accused Quintus Mucius of having been bribed to hinder the voting in the Tribal Assembly and to obstruct the oversight of the Senate in the Roman Republic. He hinted that Crassus and Caesar were supplying Catiline, Antonius, and their followers with lavish funds for bribing the electorate. He went so far as to accuse Crassus of being the instigator of the "Pisonian Conspiracy," thus making Catiline appear as a brutish tool under the influence of a much more powerful, wealthy, and dangerous *popularis*.

This speech had a devastating effect upon the senatorial *nobiles*. They may not have believed everything that Cicero had said, but he had revealed so much and in such a convincing manner that there was little doubt to whom the majority of their votes would now go. Catiline responded abusively, belittling Cicero as an out-of-town upstart, but to no avail. The tide of opinion had been turned; the final blow to his chances for election had been sharply and eloquently struck by the tongue of Cicero. The latter, although only an equestrian by birth, was the safest and most obvious choice for the *optimates* to back. Their support, combined with his backing from the *equites* and the Pompeian *populares*, gave him the combination of votes he needed to win the consular election. Thus, when polling day came, the votes of Cicero's conservative coalition victoriously lifted him into the coveted consulship. Since the four other candidates had melted into the background during the fiery race, the second consulship would have to be filled by either Catiline or Antonius—the lesser of two evils. Catiline had just been publicly branded as a dangerous revolutionary, a vile profligate, and a man with a penchant for homicide. Beside this description, his patrician lineage seemed to be of little account. Antonius, while a rather undistinguished fellow, was recognized as the type of "man who, of himself, would probably not take the lead either for good or for ill, but would add strength to another who took the lead." Antonius, therefore, seemed safer to the voters, and was chosen as the other consul of the republic for the year 63.[11]

Cicero had attained the office to which most Roman senatorial politicians aspired. He was soon to be one of the consuls of Rome, the supreme magistrates of the republic. Catiline, on the other hand, had been shut out of the position which he felt was his by birthright. He had been publicly slandered and then beaten at the polls by the man to whom he derisively referred as *inquilinus* ("the lodger"). This former equestrian from a small town had been the first *homo novus* in decades to obtain the consulship, and at his expense no less! Catiline had gone deeply into debt trying to gain the position. He had counted on winning the consulship and subsequently holding a rich provincial post where he might gather a golden harvest and come back to Italy to live in splendor like other patrician potentates. But he had failed. He was defeated, disgraced, and more deeply in debt than ever before. He was floundering. He intended to obtain supreme power in the republic in one way or another, and that malicious-tongued "new man" was not going to stop him. If he could get power legally, so much the better; if not, he would take it by force. Therefore, during the following year he worked intensively to build up a strong following among all of the discontented elements of Italian society. His primary goal would be to win the consular election of the following summer. If he failed in this endeavor, he would have the support needed to lead a revolution by force. Yet, for the time being, his intrigues would have to take a back seat to the machinations of Crassus, Caesar, and their agents in the *populares* faction.[12]

After the election, Crassus seems to have withdrawn his support from Catiline. The latter had failed in his two bids for the consulship and had not proved to be as amenable to direction as the great financier had hoped. Such radical utterances as "debt cancellation" and "proscription of the rich" certainly could not be condoned by one of Rome's wealthiest creditors. Crassus was still hoping to find some way to strengthen his position before Pompey returned victoriously from the East at the head of loyal troops. He remembered only too vividly how Sulla had come back to proscribe his political enemies. If Pompey were to repeat the actions of his predecessor, Crassus knew that his own name would probably head the list. After all, had he not been the bitter rival of Pompey since the days of Sulla? Was not his wealth an ideal target for a proscription? What he needed and had been trying to gain was enough power and support to assure himself of a strong bargaining position by the time Pompey returned. He knew that one of Pompey's first concerns would be land for his veterans. Thus, he concocted a scheme to get control of all available public land in Italy. He could not expect to get his plan introduced by the consular office as Cicero was bound to veto any radical measure which Antonius might try to initiate. So, he turned to the trusty weapon of the *populares*—the tribunate.

In December of 64, one of the tribunes, Publius Servilius Rullus, was induced to propose an agrarian bill of unprecedented scope. Its nominal purpose was to provide land grants in Italy and the provinces for the landless crowd of citizens in Rome. However, the proposed means of carrying out this exemplary project revealed that concern for the poor was not the only motive behind it. Most of the land planned for distribution was supposed to be Italian, but very little of the *ager publicus populi Romani* was still available on the peninsula. It would therefore be necessary to raise large sums of money with which the purchase of unoccupied land could be carried out. A powerful ten-man commission was to be set up to procure the needed funds and to purchase and distribute the land. It was the extensive powers that were to be granted to the land commission which made the measure seem so dangerous. The commission was empowered to sell all public lands at home and abroad and to take money from the state treasury in order to acquire the necessary funds. It could establish colonies in Italy or the provinces as it saw fit, and it could levy and maintain as many soldiers as were needed to carry out and enforce its decisions. By the terms of this proposal, the commission would seemingly have control over the newly conquered lands of Pompey as well as the revenue which he would bring back for the treasury. It could conceivably also use its *imperium* ("right of command") to raise an army and occupy Egypt, which had been bequeathed to Rome in the will of a late pharaoh. By dominating this commission, Crassus would have military forces, the state treasury, public lands, and possibly even a new province under his control when Pompey came back from his Eastern command. He would be in an excellent bargaining position, and Pompey would have little chance of setting up a dictatorship and proscribing his political enemies short of civil war. The agrarian bill had a good chance for passage as land distribution was always popular with the city mob and poor voters in the *Comitia Tributa*. Antonius, the political ally of Crassus, expected to be named to the commission, and he was planning to give his support to the measure when he assumed his consulship in January of 63.[13]

To Cicero and the interests he represented, the Rullan land bill was anathema. As it appeared to undermine the interests of Pompey, many equestrians and the Pompeian *populares* were vehemently opposed to it. Since it also seemed to undercut senatorial prerogatives in finance and foreign affairs, the *optimates* were not favorably disposed to it either. They were not pleased with the increasing power of Pompey, but on the other hand, they did not wish to see a rival *popularis* subvert the republican constitution even more while the general was away. Such a development could quite possibly lead to civil war when Pompey returned, which could result in the establishment of a dictatorship and further proscriptions. Optimate leaders such as Catulus, Lucullus, and Cato, were opposed to such a prospect. They wished to strengthen the position of the Senate in the absence of Pompey, and thus would resist any radical plans which might subvert senatorial power.

Cicero, a firm believer in republican institutions, was also opposed to the designs of the radical *populares*. Although he now certainly considered himself one of the "best men," he was also a spokesman for moderate equestrian and popular Pompeian interests. So, at the same time that he did not wish to see the authority of the Senate diminished, neither did he desire to see the Italian *equites* and the Pompeian *populares* slighted by senatorial *optimates*. He had been elected by a combination of support from all three of these elements and was expected to champion the interests of each. Therefore, he wished to gather them into a united alliance against dangerous radicals like Crassus, Caesar, and Catiline. He successfully carried out this design during his consulship, bringing together what he called a *coniunctio bonorum omnium* ("a coalition of all good men"), which enabled him to defeat the radical measures and revolutionary designs of his opponents.[14]

The first struggle for Cicero as consul would be against the Rullan land bill; but even before he entered office, he struck a crippling blow to the radicals. He was a good judge of character, and he knew that his fellow consul's chief interest was self-interest and that his chief need was more money to pay off his debts. As Cicero had drawn a rich provincial assignment (Macedonia), and Antonius a poor one (Gaul) for their proconsular governorships, he had a tool for bargaining which he used most astutely. He immediately offered to exchange assignments with Antonius if the latter would agree to support him "in defense of their country," which in essence meant following whatever line of policy Cicero should take. Antonius, who was known to be a supporter not only of the Rullan measure, but also a political ally of Catiline, was wise enough to judge that a sure thing was better than a hazardous hope. Thus, he switched his allegiance from the radical *populares* to the conservative coalition of Cicero.[15]

When Cicero began his consulship on 1 January 63 BC, he was therefore backed by Antonius in opposition to the land bill. He swiftly attacked the measure in several speeches in the Senate and in the Forum, revealing the true intents and purposes of its promoters. By some rather clever oratory, he performed the difficult feat of turning the common people against the bill even though it had been professedly brought forward in their interests. He compared the dreary toil of the farm to the exciting life in the city with its entertainments, political contests, corn doles, etc.

and won them over to his side. The news that Pompey had returned from the Caucasus to Syria must also have added strength to the arguments of Cicero against the measure. Having lost much of the popular support for the bill, and with the shadow of Pompey stretching closer to Italy, Rullus and Crassus withdrew the land proposal even before a vote could be taken on it in the *comitia*.[16]

As Crassus was directly identified with no more anti-Pompeian or anti-optimate activities in the following year, it was probable that he nervously resigned himself to wait quietly and see what course of action his rival would take upon his return. Crassus had failed in all his efforts over the past two years to gain a strong position against Pompey through radical means. He thus discontinued these activities and took on the demeanor of a "solid citizen." Many nobles of both popular and optimate sympathies were indebted to him for loans. He apparently hoped that these associations and his cessation from radical schemes would shield him from the enmity of Pompey. It was in this position of "solid citizen" that he was to perform an invaluable service for Cicero in the latter's upcoming struggle with Catiline.

Though Crassus disentangled himself from anti-optimate legislation, he most probably did not discontinue his support of Julius Caesar. The latter was definitely a valuable friend to have as he was popular with the urban mob and on good terms with Pompey. Caesar may have been connected with the Rullan measure in regard to the annexation of Egypt; but with Pompey now in a position to march swiftly upon Egypt or to sail promptly to Italy, his subsequent activities were strictly anti-optimate. In this way, he could increase his own stature at optimate expense, but without running the risk of alienating Pompey. Caesar planned to run for the praetorship in the summer election, and thus launched an anti-optimate campaign especially intended to strengthen his backing among the old Marian supporters. There were three tribunicial proposals with which he may have been connected: One would have lifted the ban on holding public offices from the sons of men proscribed by Sulla; another would have reinstated in the Senate Autronius and Sulla, the consuls-elect ousted by bribery in 66, and granted them the right to seek the office again; and a third would have effected a remission or reduction of debts. Cicero, however, fresh from his triumph over the Rullan land bill, was able to lead the conservative coalition to a quick victory over these unsettling proposals.[17]

Caesar was assuredly unhappy at the defeat of these measures, but he was probably even more disturbed at the strength which the *optimates* were gaining behind the oratory of Cicero. The latter's influence with the common people was detrimental to *populares* activities and was making the Senate's position too strong for Caesar's liking. Up until this time, Caesar's offensives against the oligarchy had been rather indirect and not too consequential. Now he decided to launch a bold assault upon one of the most important weapons in the arsenal of senatorial authority—a challenge to the *senatus consultum ultimum*. This "ultimate decree of the Senate" was a means of declaring martial law in times of emergency. The Senate would issue a decree proclaiming *Videant consules ne quid res publica detrimenti capiat* ("Let the consuls see that the republic suffers no harm"), presumably freeing the magistrates from responsibility for any illegal actions which they might have to commit during the time of crisis. However, this decree could be used as a weapon of suppression by the optimate-dominated Senate upon dangerous popular demagogues who seemed to be threatening its authority. The younger Gracchus, Saturninus, Glaucia, and many of their followers in the urban mob and equestrian order had lost their lives in the repressive actions employed under the sanction of the *senatus consultum ultimum* in earlier decades of the late republic. The *senatus consultum ultimum* could be a positive tool in regard to maintaining public order and protecting the constitution, but its misuse resulted in unfortunate side effects.[18]

Caesar decided to play up the deleterious side of the decree, hoping to alienate the common citizen from senatorial authority. He arranged for the tribune Titus Labienus to indict Gaius Rabirius for treason (*perduellio*). The latter was an elderly gentleman of the optimate faction who had taken part in the killing of a popular radical tribune, Lucius Saturninus, over thirty years before under the "ultimate decree." Labienus rushed a bill through the *Comitia Tributa* which set up an archaic style court composed of two judges who were authorized to investigate and pass sentence upon the defendant. It was arranged that Julius Caesar and his clan relative Lucius Caesar be named judges. They carried out the investigation and trial in such a way that the Senate and its use of the *senatus consultum ultimum* was presented in a very bad light. Poor old Rabirius, a helpless victim of circumstances, was quickly condemned by the biased judges. The Senate and its new champion Cicero obviously could not allow this dangerous challenge to their authority to go uncontested. Thus, an appeal to the *Comitia Centuriata*, the more conservative assembly, was brought forward in behalf of Rabirius with Cicero and Hortensius, Rome's most famous pleaders, serving as his defenders. Cicero brilliantly defended the legality, necessity, and utility of the *senatus consultum ultimum* and tempered the hostility of the people toward it by reminding them that the attack upon the demagogue Saturninus had been led by the great popular leader Marius himself. None the less, as the verdict was in doubt, an optimate praetor, Metellus Celer, ran over to the Janiculum Hill across the Tiber River and in an archaic action pulled down the military flag, which automatically dissolved the assembly before a vote could be taken. What the verdict would have been is difficult to say, since the sources differ in their appraisal of Rabirius' chances. But the mere fact that Caesar did not press the issue further gave a victory to the *optimates*. The sympathy aroused for the hapless old senator and the eloquence of the defense offered by Cicero had seemingly neutralized Caesar's attack and focused attention upon the necessity of the Senate's most potent weapon. The position and power of the Senate had been little damaged by the trial. In vindicating the use of the *senatus consultum ultimum* in emergency situations, Cicero preserved a constitutional instrument that he would shortly need not merely for the protection of senatorial authority, but truly for the defense of the fabric of Roman society. Yet, Caesar also emerged from the trial in a better position than when he had entered it. He had presented himself as a popular leader deeply concerned for the rights of the common man against oppressive action by the senatorial oligarchy—specifically in regard to the rule that Roman citizens should not be put to death without a trial. Although the legality and the necessity of the "ultimate decree" had been defended by Cicero, Caesar had performed the equally important function of warning the Senate not to misuse it for partisan political purposes.[19]

That Caesar's popularity was not impaired by his participation in the Rabirian trial was revealed by the fact that he was shortly elected to his first important position—that of *pontifex maximus*. By obtaining this sacred office (admittedly with a generous amount of bribery), he received all the dignity and power to which the "chief priest" of the Roman state religion was entitled. Caesar was a superb politician and had an uncanny ability to make the right move at the right time. He was wise enough to see that Cicero's conservative coalition was now in effective control of Roman politics. All but one of the measures introduced by *popularis* tribunes had been defeated by the coalition of Cicero. Caesar himself had come out of the Rabirian incident somewhat successful, but certainly second best (Rabirius had been allowed to go free). His only success had been in the quasi-political race for the chief priesthood. Therefore, he decided to temper his activities and cease from making any more overt assaults upon optimate interests. He may have done so in order to disassociate his name from the subversive activities of his popular faction ally Catiline. Caesar was now in as strong a position as he could expect under the circumstances. He was definitely popular with the urban mob and held the impressive title of *pontifex maximus*. There was no reason to jeopardize his position by association with the radical Catiline. Caesar knew when to pull his punches; Catiline did not.[20]

As the consular election of 63 neared, Cicero and his forces had successfully met and overcome the challenges of the radical *populares*. Crassus had been defeated and Caesar neutralized—at least for a time. The conservative coalition seemed stronger than ever, and an unaccustomed stability had emerged in the political atmosphere. Yet, this was only the quiet before the storm as Catiline was soon to burst upon the scene with some of the most revolutionary designs ever conjured by the mind of a Roman citizen.

Illustration 2 Bust of Pompey (Capitoline Museum, Rome).

Illustration 3   Statue of Cicero the Orator (Palazzo di Giustizia, Rome).

Illustration 4   Aerial of Rome over the Colosseum to the Forum (Rome).

Illustration 5   View of the Roman Forum with the Senate House and Assembly area where Cicero spoke against Catiline (Rome).

Illustration 6   Cicero delivering the *Oratio in Catilinam* I (Fresco of Cesare Maccari in the Palazzo Madama Ora del Senato, Rome).

Illustration 7 View to the ruins of the bathhouse at Catiline's Etruscan base in Faesulae (Fiesole).

Illustration 8 Aerial over the Etruscan hills where Catiline's army marched out to do battle at Pistoria (Tuscany).

Illustration 9   View of Cicero's route down the *Via Sacra* in the Forum after he had put the urban conspirators to death (Rome).

Illustration 10   Bust of Cicero the Statesman (Capitoline Museum, Rome).

Illustration 11   Statue of Caesar the Proconsul (Capitoline City Council Chamber, Rome).

V The Conspiracy of Catiline

"The absence of the Roman armies in the uttermost quarters of the world . . . induced Catiline to entertain the nefarious design of overthrowing his country."

Florus, *Epitomae* II. 12. 1

As Crassus and Caesar were temporarily stymied and Pompey was off in the East, Catiline remained the only popular leader of any consequence ready and willing to combat the resurgent optimate forces. And he was the most dangerous *popularis* leader of all, since he was amenable to employing any means in order to obtain the position, power, and wealth he desired.[1]

That Catiline hankered after power so desperately is no surprise. He was the scion of an ancient patrician clan and was inclined by birth and tradition to seek and serve in the highest offices of the republic. By natural disposition he was ambitious, aggressive, and avaricious—a man accustomed to taking what he wanted when he wanted, whether it be the property of provincial subjects or the lives and fortunes of fellow citizens. His family heritage and basic personality prevented him from gracefully retiring to his estates after he had been defeated in the consular election of 64. The humiliating frustration of that defeat grieved him greatly during the following year and deepened his desire for power all the more. He felt that his *dignitas* had been wronged, that an unworthy man had been promoted to the position which he himself deserved. He loathed the *inquilinus* who had dared to slander him in public and defeat him at the polls. Likewise, he came to despise the optimate clique and their prosperous equestrian allies for supporting the acid-tongued *homo novus*. He was infused with jealous envy of the senatorial *nobiles*, who to him seemed to possess "influence, power, office, and wealth" while he was left with "danger, defeat, prosecutions and poverty." Catiline was determined to change this situation, and he perceived that the means for doing so were at hand.[2]

Within the radical wing of the *populares* there were many senatorial politicians like Catiline who were plagued with debts and inflamed by jealousy of the principal *optimates*. Indeed, as Plutarch later commented, some "men of the highest reputation and spirit had beggared themselves on shows, feasts, and the pursuit of office" only to have their efforts obstructed by the solid phalanx of the *boni*. These men outside the inner clique of senatorial leadership were as disposed toward change as was Catiline. Sallust remarked that they "would rather see the state embroiled than accept their own exclusion from political power."[3]

At this time the metropolis of Rome was a gathering place for dispossessed or ruined peasant farmers from several areas of rural Italy. This phenomenon increased the chronic instability of the chaotic politics in the capital. Among the restless urban mob there were many malcontents who "hated the established order and desired innovation."[4]

There was also much discontent throughout the country districts of Italy. The confiscations of Sulla had left some small farmers bitter at the loss of their land. Many of the veteran soldiers who had displaced those farmers had failed to make good in their agrarian life, had gone into debt, and were "looking back regretfully to the loot which past victories had brought them." They were seemingly ready to join with other debt-ridden farmers in a revolt against the present regime and its harsh debt laws. The region around Faesulae in the hills of Etruria north of Rome where many of the Sullan veterans were located was the most dangerous area of all.[5]

Likewise, out in the provinces of the empire there were many subject peoples who were not happy with Roman rule. They objected to the oppression practiced by some of their optimate governors and to the harsh tax-farming methods employed by the equestrian *publicani*. The powerful Celtic tribe of the Allobroges in Transalpine Gaul was especially discontent at this time.[6]

These discontented groups had little chance for their grievances to be redressed unless they could be brought together in a common front. Catiline saw in this possibility his means to obtaining power. He would become the champion of the wretched and the leader of the oppressed; and backed by these disaffected groups, he would defeat Cicero's conservative coalition and rise to the pinnacle of power. Therefore, during the year after his election defeat, he concentrated upon strengthening and widening his support for the upcoming consular campaign in the summer of 63. He already had considerable backing among the dissolute and poverty-stricken politicians of the capital. Now with Crassus and Caesar unwilling to commit themselves to further dangerous maneuvers, Catiline offered himself as the leader of those radical *populares* who through need and/or disposition felt inclined to move against the regime before Pompey's return. Catiline was not the least hesitant in encouraging these malcontents with the kind of promises they wanted to hear.

His bold, forceful, and generous manner was also attractive to the impressionable youth of the city. Dissatisfied with the status quo, many were easily brought under the sway of the fiery revolutionary. Catiline did his utmost to widen this following, believing that they would be very useful to his designs. He also attempted to firm up his support among the Sullan veterans in Etruria. This restless lot was led by Gaius Manlius, a man "who had served with distinction under Sulla" and was a strong backer of Catiline. The latter raised money on his own credit or on that of his friends and sent it to Manlius, who had agreed to campaign for Catiline and bring a strong contingent of rural voters to Rome for the upcoming consular election.[7]

The immediate goal of Catiline was to obtain power legally through winning the consulship in the Centuriate Assembly elections in the summer of 63. If he failed in this final election bid, he would take revolutionary measures to gain his ends illegally with the help of his election supporters. During the summer campaign, he styled himself as the *dux et signifer calamitosorum* ("the general and standard-bearer of the unfortunate") and proffered a radical program which was bound to appeal to his disaffected followers. He promised his most important backers in a secret meeting that if he were elected, they would receive "a cancellation of debts, a proscription of the rich, offices, priesthoods, plunder, and all the other spoils that war and the license of victors can offer." His campaign was thus a virtual war on property and the existing regime which controlled it.[8]

Cicero and the conservative coalition behind him undeniably dreaded the thought of Catiline being elected consul. Yet, they had little in the way of candidates with whom to oppose him. Indeed, only three men were running against the fiery radical, and none of these was particularly outstanding. Servius Sulpicius was from old noble stock, but his family had not distinguished itself lately. He had earned some fame through the courts; but unlike Cicero, he was at a loss as a campaigner and soon alienated the senatorial class as well as the populace. Decimus Junius Silanus was not too well known and had already sustained a defeat two years earlier. The third candidate was Lucius Licinius Murena. He had served with distinction under Lucullus in the war against Mithridates, and he had won general popularity with the urban mob through the lavish games he had presented during his praetorship. Although there were no consulships in his family history, he nevertheless seemed to be the strongest opponent of Catiline among the oligarchy and the people.[9]

Since Catiline was employing a good deal of bribery to buttress his campaign, Murena also began to increase the extent of his generosity to gain supporters. Sulpicius, though having little chance of being elected, was an upright citizen and abhorred the corrupt campaign practices of his opponents. He therefore demanded that a law with harsher penalties against electoral bribery than those of the *Lex Calpurnia* be enacted. Cicero saw in this move a possible means of restraining the flagrant abuses of Catiline. He himself led the move for a new campaign practices law and swiftly managed to get one passed with a provision "that banishment for ten years should be added . . . to the penalties established for bribery." He apparently expected that the mere threat of another prosecution would preclude any further bribery on the part of Catiline.[10]

Cicero certainly needed something to slow down Catiline's campaign, since the radical candidate had gathered enough malcontents in Rome to make his election seem quite probable. He was campaigning with the utmost confidence and was often beheld

bold and happy, accompanied by a crowd of youths, protected by informers and assassins, . . . and surrounded by an army of settlers from

Arretium and Faesulae—a mob with here and there men of a very different type afflicted by the disaster of Sulla's regime. His countenance was so full of madness, his eyes of crime, his speech of arrogance that it seemed as if he had already hunted out the consulship and locked it up in his home.

Sulpicius threatened Catiline with prosecution under the new law, but to little avail; and when Marcus Porcius Cato announced in the Senate that he too was planning to bring Catiline to trial for electoral abuses, the latter brazenly retorted that "if his plans were set afire, he would extinguish the conflagration not with water, but with a general ruin." This statement inflamed the *optimates* and their allies, but Sulpicius really threw grease onto the fire when he indicated that he was even intending to prosecute Murena for campaign abuses. This was a foolish move on the part of Sulpicius, for by trying to vilify the man who was not only his but also Catiline's strongest opponent he outraged the forces of the conservative coalition. And rightly so, for by impairing Murena's chances at the polls, he was increasing those of Catiline. By this inane action, Sulpicius lost what little chance he might have had in the electoral campaign.[11]

Since Cicero was backing Silanus and Murena, he felt that the inopportune action of Sulpicius was most dangerous. Information soon reached him which made this feeling all the more urgent. Catiline knew that Cicero had proposed the new bribery law with the purpose of harming his campaign. He had by then completely lost patience with Cicero's obstructions and decided that the time had come to get rid of the bothersome consul. In a meeting with his closest supporters, he designed a plan to stage a riot at the polls during which Cicero and some of his colleagues were to be slain. Fortunately for Cicero, he got word of the heinous plot the day before the polling was to be held. Cicero swiftly called the Senate into emergency session and had it vote to postpone the election. On the next day, the senators questioned Catiline about his secret promises and dangerous designs. Instead of defending himself, he shocked the senators with this audacious reply:

> What dreadful thing am I doing when there are two bodies in the state, one frail and with a weak head, and the other sturdy but without a head, if I myself become a head for the latter?

He was referring to the "haves" and "have-nots" of Roman society—the wealthy coalition behind Cicero and the poor dissidents in his following. Having spoken thus, he strode boldly out of the Senate, leaving behind the groans of concerned *optimates*.[12]

Catiline's performance certainly confirmed the intention of the majority of the Senate not to vote for him. Nevertheless, it did not pass a *senatus consultum ultimum*, as Cicero might have wished in these circumstances. Apparently, some of the senators believed that Cicero's accusation against

Catiline of intended murders at the election polls might be just another one of the consul's dramatic "last minute" appeals to sway opinion against his political enemy—as he had done a year previously in the *Oratio in Toga Candida*. The trial of Rabirius by Caesar had made the Senate hesitant to employ the "ultimate decree" except in manifest cases of national emergency. So, the senators let the matter pass without action. The inaction of the Senate was, of course, very disquieting to Cicero. His own life was in danger, and the urban poor seemed favorably disposed to the candidacy of Catiline. Something had to be done to insure his own safety and to defeat Catiline's election bid. If the Senate would not act as a body, the consul would have to take action of his own.

Cicero therefore assembled a strong bodyguard of supporters and attendants who would accompany him to the *Campus Martius*, the "field of Mars" to the north of the city where the Centuriate Assembly elections were held. This precaution would protect his own person, but it might not swing the electorate against Catiline. What Cicero needed was a dramatic incident that would arouse the populace against his enemy. As a master showman, he knew how to handle the people as few politicians did. He thus arranged the following maneuvers. Men were sent about the city spreading rumors that the life of the consul was being threatened by Catiline and his supporters. The urban mob undoubtedly liked the program of the radical Catiline and assuredly reveled in his brassy manner and impudent flouting of the *optimates*. However, they also respected the "new man," who had made it to the consulship through his own merits and was the spokesman for their popular hero Pompey; they may have favored Catiline, but they did not want to see any harm befall Cicero. The master stroke of Cicero was the manner in which he entered the *campus*. He came surrounded by his strong bodyguard and was girded with a "broad and conspicuous breastplate" that everyone could see. The rumors about his danger were thereby confirmed in the minds of the citizens. These maneuvers had the desired results: Catiline's men did not dare to attack the well-guarded consul, and enough of the voters were aroused against Catiline to insure the election of Silanus and Murena. Mainly by the efforts of Cicero, Catiline had again lost a bid to obtain power through the consulship.[13]

The unsuccessful campaign left Catiline plagued with debts, angered by repeated defeats, and distraught with unfulfilled desires. Three times he had endeavored to win the consulship by election; three times "the establishment" had thwarted him. As he could not attain power through legal means, he now turned to the revolutionary plan of seizing power by force. His election supporters would be the means to carry out this course of action, since they were almost as anxious as he to overturn the existing political structure. The situation in Italy was favorable for a revolution as there were few armed troops stationed on the peninsula: Most of the legions were far off in the East with Pompey. Yet, as the latter's Eastern campaigns were drawing to a close, Catiline and his followers needed to seize control of Rome and Italy as quickly and efficiently as possible.[14]

Sometime shortly after the summer elections, Catiline gathered his staunchest supporters together and expressed his desire to lead them in a conspiracy to gain control of the republic. He laid before them the attractive proposals of debt cancellation, land redistribution, and the acquisition of the power and wealth that the optimate clique had prevented them from obtaining. These suggestions were most attractive to the profligate, needy, and rash-spirited associates of the radical *popularis*. Although many of them had renowned family names and held senatorial membership, most of them were deeply in debt on account of the extravagant expenditures which characterized their lives. A listing of their names and activities reads like a "rogues' gallery" of recent Roman politics. Publius Cornelius Lentulus, a man of distinguished birth, held the dubious honor of being a praetor for the second time. He had served as a consul in the year 71 but subsequently had been expelled from the Senate because of the infamous licentiousness of his public and private life. He had been forced to run for and hold the praetorship again in order to regain senatorial dignity. Gaius Cassius Cethegus, a senator of praetorian rank, was well known for his impatient and rash nature and had an obsession for collecting dangerous weapons. Publius Autronius Paetus, also of praetorian rank, had been elected to the consulship for 65 but had been tried and convicted of corrupt election practices and thus prevented from taking office. He was rumored to have been a participant in the abortive "Pisonian Conspiracy" with Catiline back in the winter of 66/65. And Lucius Cassius Longinus, a corpulent debauchee who had been an unsuccessful candidate for the consulship in 64, had a propensity for villainous deeds, especially incendiarism. Other senators who graced this "elite company" with their aid and counsel were Publius and Servius Sulla, the sons of Servius Sulla, Lucius Vargunteius, Quintus Annius, Marcus Porcius Laeca, Lucius Bestia, and Quintus Curius. Discontented equestrians among the group included Marcus Fulvius Nobilior, Lucius Statilius, Publius Gabinius Capito, and Gaius Cornelius. Allied to these were "many members of local nobility from the Italian colonies and municipalities."[15]

The bonds of union for the conspirators were debt, defeat, frustration, desire for change, and a common faith in the abilities of Catiline to lead them to a better status. Therefore, they readily accepted Catiline's proposals and swore an oath to remain faithful to the conspiracy, which he called "a great and noble enterprise." Though it hardly seems believable, it was reported by several ancient sources that this oath was sealed with the drinking of human blood mixed with wine—and that this abominable brew was obtained from the veins of a youth specially sacrificed for this ceremony.[16]

The conspiracy that Catiline had outlined to his accomplices was of a twofold nature. There were to be military rebellions through the country districts of Italy and a concurrent violent uprising in Rome. Aware of the careers of Marius, Sulla, and Pompey, Catiline realized that he would need military support both to gain and to retain power. Therefore, late in the summer he advised his chief rural assistant Manlius to start forming the Sullan veterans of Etruria into fighting bands. Since these famous plunderers were Catiline's staunchest backers, the work progressed quickly. In order to organize support among discontented veterans and farmers in other portions of Italy, he sent "a certain Septimius of Camerinum (Camerino) to Picenum; Gaius Julius to Apulia; and others to various districts where he thought that each would be serviceable to his project." While these actions were being carried out over the peninsula, Catiline and his chief assistant in the city, Lentulus, were planning the insurrection for the capital. Their strategy called for the murder of the consuls and the leaders of the conservative coalition, simultaneous acts of arson in several parts of the city, and the occupation of strategic points with armed men. Thus, the overall plan of this pernicious plot was to stage several military revolts across Italy that would be followed almost immediately by a violent insurrection in Rome. The external rebellions were to be initiated by Manlius on 27 October while the internal sedition was to take place on the following day. By means of these rebellions, centered in and directed from Rome, Catiline and his comrades would become the masters of Italy. The power and wealth that they so desperately desired would be theirs.[17]

However, Catiline and his fellow conspirators still had to reckon with Cicero. The sagacious consul knew that the radical *popularis* was not a man to be taken lightly, and he had been suspicious of his designs ever since their heated electoral battle during the summer of 64. Cicero had again prevented his enemy from winning the consulship in 63, but he hardly expected that a man of Catiline's proud and daring nature would acquiesce in defeat. Therefore, Cicero remained alert and tried to monitor the activities of Catiline and his followers. From reports of various contacts on the peninsula, he knew that some dangerous actions were being planned, but he was probably unsure of the overall design of the *coniuratio Catilinae*.

Fortuna must have been smiling upon the vigilant consul, as he was soon made cognizant of the full extent and detailed plans of the conspiracy from an unlikely source. One of the conspirators was Quintus Curius. He, like Lentulus, was a disgraced politician who had been expelled from the Senate on account of his openly shameful conduct. As he had fallen more heavily into debt, he had not been able to favor his mistress Fulvia with the lavish gifts to which she had become accustomed. Not wanting to lose her affections, he promised that soon he would be a rich man and would be able to give her anything she desired. Fulvia was curious and hounded him to tell her what he meant by this bragging until he divulged information about the schemes of Catiline. The patriotism of Fulvia was apparently of a higher caliber than her morals; so, because of the dangerous nature of the insidious conspiracy, she felt constrained to inform the consul. Cicero realized that the word of a conspirator's mistress was not enough to employ in a public disclosure of the plot; but he reasoned that she could be most useful in his efforts to keep abreast of the actions of Catiline and his fellow plotters. Therefore, he persuaded Fulvia to employ her influence—along with a substantial monetary contribution, which he supplied—to induce Curius to act as his spy and keep him appraised of the conspirators' activities.[18]

Cicero certainly would have taken steps to avert the upcoming sedition even if he had not received evidence acceptable for public disclosure. But the kind of information he needed soon arrived from a former supporter of Catiline. On the night of 20 October, an unknown messenger left a packet of letters at the home of the great financier and politician Marcus Crassus. One was intended for Crassus himself while the others were addressed to various members of the Senate. Crassus opened only his own, which "told him that there was to be much bloodshed caused by Catiline, and advised him to escape secretly from the city." Crassus was alarmed by this message because he knew that if Catiline were successful in his dangerous designs, Pompey would swiftly return from the East with his powerful legions and certainly be able to crush the conspirators in a civil war. A proscription would probably follow in which he would head the list, as he would be suspected of complicity in the sedition on account of his past association with Catiline. Crassus undoubtedly wanted to avert this danger. So, he called together some of the other nobles to whom the letters were addressed (Metellus Scipio and Marcus Marcellus among them) and consulted them on the matter. They all agreed that Cicero should be informed. Without waiting for morning, they went to the house of the consul, awoke him in the middle of the night, and showed him the letters. With these written messages, Cicero now had the hard evidence he needed to take action. He decided to convene the Senate in the morning and lay this information before it. The author of these letters was not known as they were unsigned. Catiline himself might have sent them because he was indebted to Crassus for past help and still had several friends among the nobility not included in the ranks of the conspirators. He may have wanted to protect these individuals by warning them in advance. However, he was not the type of man to let sentiment stand in the way of his desires. Thus, one of the other conspirators may have sent the letters for the same reasons, since Catiline's supporters were not as single-minded, strong-willed, or vicious as he was. In any case, the letters were an unexpected godsend to Cicero.[19]

On the morning of 21 October, Cicero convened an emergency meeting of the Senate. He announced that he had knowledge of a nefarious conspiracy that was about to burst forth and wreak havoc upon the republic. He reported that Manlius was going to start a rebellion in the country districts on 27 October and that Catiline was going to stage a sedition in the capital on the following day. He then produced the packet of letters given to him the night before and declared that they would provide sufficient evidence to substantiate his serious allegations. He handed the letters to the men to whom they were addressed and requested that the contents of each be read aloud. This was done, and "all alike were found to tell of the conspiracy." When Quintus Arrius, a senator of praetorian rank, reported that Manlius was mustering troops in Etruria, the senators were convinced that Cicero's imputations were true. The Senate as a body rallied to Cicero's suggestion that drastic measures were needed to meet this serious threat to the stability of the state. The *senatus consultum ultimum* was passed stating that "the consuls should take heed that the republic might not suffer any harm" (*darent operam consules ne quid res publica detrimenti caperet*). With the "ultimate decree," Cicero felt that he now had the weapon he needed to defend the republic against its desperate enemies. Under this senatorial declaration of martial law, he and his associate consul Antonius could "levy troops and conduct war, apply unlimited force to citizens and allies alike, and exercise unlimited jurisdiction and command at home and abroad."[20]

Cicero swung into action immediately: He commissioned Quintus Metellus with the task of defending Rome outside the walls while he handled the precautions within the city. Metellus was the outstanding commander of the optimate faction at that time and was waiting outside the gates for a triumph. He had recently completed the successful conquest and subjugation of Crete, for which endeavor he had received the cognomen *Creticus*. He and his troops prepared to obstruct any rebel attacks outside of the capital. Within the gates Cicero arranged for armed guards to attend himself and other important officials and established garrisons throughout the city. Because of these preparations the conspirators were unable to carry out their sedition in Rome on the scheduled day.[21]

During this period Catiline played the role of the injured innocent—the maligned patrician whom Cicero had chosen as his favorite "whipping boy." And when nothing happened on 28 October, people began to doubt the authenticity of the letters which Cicero had produced as evidence. They probably wondered if the *homo novus* was just trying to glorify himself by pretending to have saved the state from great danger that actually existed nowhere but in his own ambitious mind. Then, at the end of the month, a senator by the name of Lucius Saenius reported that Manlius had indeed "taken the field with a large army on 27 October" in the vicinity of Faesulae in north central Italy. Other senators told of rumors about suspicious activities in Capua and Apulia in southern Italy. The Senate finally recognized the seriousness of the situation and passed several decrees that were meant to meet the emergency. Military commanders were sent out to various areas of Italy "with instructions to raise adequate forces to deal with the critical situation that had arisen": Quintus Marcius Rex and Quintus Metellus Celer were sent north to Faesulae and Picenum while Quintus Pompeius Rufus and Quintus Metellus Creticus were sent south to Capua and Apulia. Rewards and pardons were offered to individuals who would proffer information about the conspiracy. Orders were sent out to close the gladiatorial schools and for the gladiators to be employed as guards in endangered towns. Junior magistrates in Rome were commissioned to augment the nocturnal patrols which Cicero had instituted throughout the city.[22]

Although Catiline was by then indicted under the *Lex Plautia de vi* (the Plautian Law concerning force), there was no unequivocal evidence with which he could be convicted. He was still in the clear since he had not incited a revolt in the capital, and the rural rebellion of Manlius had not been undertaken in his name. Therefore, he continued to play the part of the guiltless patrician and ostensibly welcomed the indictment as a means of proving his innocence. He offered to entrust himself to the household of a praetor or even to that of Cicero. But the wary consul was not about to spend his nights under the same roof with his homicidal enemy, and so he sharply rejected the suggestion. Catiline probably hoped for and expected this reaction from Cicero, and thus was able to entrust himself to the much less vigilant Marcus Metellus, an old and noble friend.[23]

While pretending to be preparing for a trial, Catiline was actually promoting his conspiratorial plans. However, the situation must not have looked propitious, for he had been unable to carry out his murderous designs in the city, and Manlius had begun the rural rebellion without realizing that the urban part of the plot had been obstructed. When news reached Catiline that the nocturnal attempt to seize Praeneste on the first of November had failed, he perceived that a change of plans and a tightening up of the conspiratorial organization needed be arranged immediately.[24]

Catiline thereupon sent messages to the leading conspirators that they should meet secretly on the evening of 6 November at the home of Marcus Porcius Laeca. Eluding the nocturnal street patrols, each of the plotters made his way to the street of the scythe-makers where the abode of Laeca was located. When all had arrived, Catiline began the meeting by upbraiding them for the indolent and timorous quality of their recent actions. He reminded them of their solemn oath, and he enumerated the many penalties they would suffer if detected as compared to the many advantages they would obtain if successful in their great conspiracy. He stirred their courage with vigorous incitements to action and then discussed the best means of carrying out their perilous designs. It was decided that he would soon leave to take command of the rebel forces in Etruria because the situation in Rome was becoming too dangerous for him. It was agreed that Autronius would go with him while the other leading conspirators would remain behind to direct the sedition within the capital. Lentulus, the highest-ranking conspirator because of his earlier consulship, was to assume direction of the insurrection at Rome. Cethegus was to manage the massacre of the senators while Cassius was placed in charge of the arson teams that were to start fires throughout the city. Others were assigned to plunder the treasury. When the urban uprising had been initiated and Rome was engulfed in confusion, Catiline was to march hastily toward it with his forces from the country districts in order to take control by force and stamp out any resistance which might be encountered. It was a well-thought-out plan which would have completely overturned "the establishment." Rome would have fallen easy prey to the army of Catiline arriving at the opportune moment. Yet Catiline complained that an important task remained to be carried out before he departed. Cicero, the one man who had obstructed all their previous designs, still stood in the way of their victory. Therefore, Catiline resolved that the hindersome consul must be murdered before he left for Etruria. Two of the more audacious members of the group—the senator Lucius Vargunteius and the equestrian Gaius Cornelius—volunteered for this necessary deed and promised to slay the vexatious magistrate before dawn. When all present understood their assignments and comprehended the gravity of the situation, the meeting was adjourned with each of the conspiratorial leaders holding the highest hopes for the success of their daring venture.[25]

The Catilinarian Conspiracy had now entered its final and most dangerous stages. The actions of Cicero during the next month in combating this grave danger to the republic would bring him to the height of his political career and assure him a lasting place among the world's greatest orators.

VI The Victory of Cicero

> "As Cicero passed through the Forum to his house . . ., the citizens
> . . . shouted and clapped, calling him the savior and founder of his
> country."
>
> Plutarch, *Cicero* 22. 3

While Catiline and his co-conspirators were secretly making their final
plans to take over the Roman Republic, Cicero was probably sleeping
soundly, unaware that his life might shortly be brought to a violent end by
the plunging daggers of his enemies.[1] It was customary in the late republic
for citizens to pay their respects to an important person by a *salutatio*—a
ceremonial morning call. Since the visitors would sometimes arrive before
their host had fully arisen, they would often be received in the bedchamber
for an audience. Vargunteius and Cornelius intended to be Cicero's earliest
visitors, hoping to find him just arising. It would thereby be much easier to
dispatch him. Fortunately for Cicero, his informer Quintus Curius was still
numbered among the inner circle of the conspiracy and had attended the
meeting at Laeca's house. As soon as the gathering had broken up, Curius
had sent his mistress Fulvia to warn the slumbering consul of the impend-
ing danger. Cicero immediately took precautionary measures to protect
himself. He summoned several officials to his home and informed them of
the plot against his life, even naming the conspirators who were to come
in the morning as his greeters. He then fortified his house with a strong
guard. As dawn broke, Vargunteius and Cornelius appeared at Cicero's
door just as he had foretold. "When they were prevented from entering,
they were incensed and made an outcry at the door," which convinced the
nobles present that Cicero was correct about the scheming of Catiline and
his followers.[2]

Catiline had planned to depart from Rome as soon as Cicero had been
slain. Although the attempted assassination on the morning of 7 November had failed, Cicero probably expected that Catiline would leave the city
on that day anyway. As his flight would make his guilt seem all the more
apparent, the consul waited until the following morning to call a meeting
of the Senate. He thereupon summoned the senators on 8 November to
the well-defended temple of *Juppiter Stator* on the Palatine Hill near the
Forum with the intention of presenting to them a full account of the absent
Catiline's conspiracy.[3]

The senators had just been called to order when Catiline strode boldly
into the temple and took a seat among them as if there was nothing to the

distressing rumors about his recent activities. Astonished at this outrageous exhibition of audacity, those near him rose to their feet and silently vacated that portion of the hall. Forsaken by all as if infected by a contagious disease, he sat alone in a forlorn corner. Then all eyes turned to the front of the room as the consul rose to speak. Cicero was alarmed and indignant at the presence of this man who only the morning before had attempted to have him killed. He glared directly at his adversary and launched into the following brilliant invective:

To what extent, O Catiline, will you continuously abuse our patience? For how long will that madness of yours mock us? To what end will your unbridled audacity swagger about as it does now? Are you not disturbed by the nocturnal garrison of the Palatine, by the patrols of the city, by the fear of the people, by the union of all good men, by the precaution of holding the Senate in this most fortified place, are you not even moved by the looks and countenances of these men present here today? Do you not perceive that your schemes are exposed? Do you not see that your conspiracy is already arrested and bound by the knowledge of all these men? Do you think that any of us is ignorant of what you did last night, the night before, of where you were, of whom you called together, or even of what schemes you concocted? O what times these are! O what morals we have! The Senate knows these things, the consul sees them; yet this man lives. Did I say lives? Nay, more, he even strides into the Senate, and partakes in the business of the state—all the while noting down and designating with his eyes each and everyone of us for murder. Yet we, brave men that we are, think that we are doing enough for the republic if we merely avoid his fury and shafts. O Catiline, you ought long ago to have been led to your death by order of the consul. That destruction which you have been planning for us ought to be cast upon you yourself.

As can be gleaned from just this brief passage, Cicero's *First Oration Against Catiline* was one of the greatest denunciatory harangues ever uttered. Cicero, standing alone before the Senate, went on to accuse Catiline in specific terms of planning revolution, murder, and conflagration—in short, of a seditious plot to overthrow the very framework of the republic. He castigated his enemy for a base and disgraceful personal life, hinting of perverse violations committed even against his own family. He then commanded his adversary "to depart from the city for since one of them did his work with words and the other with arms, it was necessary that a wall lie between them":

O Catiline, go forth to your impious and wicked war, bringing to the state the greatest of benefits, to yourself destruction and annihilation, and to those who have joined in your every wickedness and atrocity utter ruin.[4]

When Cicero had finished, Catiline attempted to defend himself by simulating innocence, by recalling his high birth and family heritage, and by deprecating Cicero; but he was swiftly silenced with the shouts of "traitor" and "assassin" from the senators. Dashing out of the meeting, he hurried home to appraise the adverse situation and determine his next move. His plot against the consul had failed, he was under indictment *de vi*, and he was considered a traitor by his fellow senators. His continued residence in Rome was nearly impossible. Yet he still had much sympathy among the city mob, Cicero had no written evidence against the urban conspirators, and Manlius had raised a force of 20,000 men in Etruria. The possibility of achieving his conspiratorial goals was still quite good.[5]

Therefore, even though Cicero had not been eliminated, Catiline determined to put into action the rest of the plans he had detailed in the secret meeting at Laeca's house: He would leave the city to take command of the rebellion in Etruria while Lentulus would assume control of the sedition within Rome. That night Catiline departed for the camp of Manlius with a substantial number of his followers. He left instructions for Lentulus, Cethegus, and his other audacious associates to add strength to their faction by whatever means possible, to bring the plots against the consul to a head, and to prepare for murder, arson, and the other horrors of war when he would lead the rebel forces against the city. Even while he was marching to Etruria Catiline continued his dissimulations of oppressed innocence. He relayed messages to members of the Senate alleging that he was going into voluntary exile at Massilia (Marseilles) because of the odium raised against him by the harsh and unjust denunciations of Cicero and his associates. In a letter to the respected former consul Quintus Lutatius Catulus, he lamented that he had been robbed of his dignity and the fruits of his toil while unworthy men had been elevated to the positions and prestige which he deserved. It was only because of this that he had been forced to become the champion of the oppressed; and thus his actions were entirely honorable.[6]

On the following morning of 9 November, Catiline's accomplices spread rumors through Rome that their leader had been unfairly driven from the city without any proof of his guilt. The urban mob became greatly excited over the conflicting stories of his innocence or guilt. Cicero accordingly went to the Forum and addressed the people in a *contio* (a public meeting) in an effort to calm their agitation. In this *Second Oration Against Catiline*, Cicero revealed to the people the treacherous schemes of the radical *popularis*, and he explained that he had driven the conspirator from the capital into open warfare so that there would be no more doubt as to the danger threatening the state. Telling the populace where Catiline had gone and whom he had taken with him, the consul assured them that he was diligently working for their safety and that he had dispatched Quintus Metellus Celer to secure Picenum and the Gallic provinces from Catiline's rebellion. He also warned the conspirators still left in the city that they had best leave as well, since he was vigilantly watching their movements and would not hesitate to take severe measures in suppressing any attempt at disorder.[7]

Catiline proceeded north by way of the Aurelian Road. He stopped for a few days in the vicinity of Arretium to confer with his lieutenant Gaius Flaminius and to supply his local supporters with arms. He then openly assumed the *fasces* and other insignia of the consular *imperium* (symbols of the chief magistrates' authority and right of command) and advanced to the camp of Manlius at Faesulae.[8]

When word reached Rome in mid-November that Catiline was indeed in Etruria with Manlius and preparing for war, the Senate took action by issuing several decrees: It declared the two rebel leaders public enemies; it offered pardons to members of the rebel forces who would lay down their arms by a specified date (except those facing capital charges); it directed the consuls to enroll troops at Rome; and it charged Cicero with guarding the capital and ordered Antonius to take the field against Catiline. These decrees had no immediate effect in arresting the conspirators' plans. In fact, the rebel armies of Catiline actually increased in size as a number of men who had not been privy to the conspiracy left Rome to join the rebellion. Among these discontents was a certain Aulus Fulvius, the son of a senatorial noble. When hearing of the departure of his son, the senator ordered that the boy be dragged back and put to death for his treasonous action.[9]

Through the next two weeks Rome was outwardly calm as Lentulus and his associates quietly prepared for the upcoming insurrection and waited while Catiline built up larger military forces north in Etruria. During this time an event occurred that exhibited the basic instability of late republican politics. Sulpicius, the defeated consular candidate, fulfilled his earlier threat to bring the consul-elect Murena to trial for corrupt election practices. Marcus Cato, the highly respected tribune-elect, supported Sulpicius in this untimely prosecution. The latter was motivated by envy of his competitor's success, while Cato was following his rigid Stoic philosophical principles concerning adherence to duty with an utter disregard for reality. Both were callously placing personal interests above the welfare of the republic; for if they were to have succeeded in convicting Murena, there might have been only one consul entering office in January to oppose the seditious rebellion against the state. Cicero and the more farsighted statesmen of the Senate were appalled at this foolhardy action in a time of severe civic crisis. The great optimate orator Hortensius volunteered to aid Cicero in the defense as did the *popularis* leader Crassus, who was by then firmly backing the government against the treasonous schemes of Catiline. Cicero's wit sparkled at its best in this defense. He derided the lackluster campaigning of Sulpicius and the unbending Stoicism of Cato most effectively. However, the clinching argument for acquittal was that the beginning of the new year was no time to have only one consul in office with the dangerous situation then prevailing. The jury was largely composed of men of property who most likely feared any change in the status quo. Thus, they rallied to Murena's cause and assured the government of continuing and effective military leadership against the revolutionary movements then astir.[10]

While Catiline was traveling around Etruria gathering and training troops and inciting towns to revolt, Lentulus was directing the conspiratorial activities in the capital. He was a man of the same character as Catiline—a spendthrift debauchee with a powerful ambition for sovereignty—and had easily been persuaded to join in the dangerous plot to seize power before Pompey returned. He actually believed that it was his destiny to rule Rome as a monarch, since he had been told by readers of the Sibylline Books (they were believed to have mystic powers of foretelling the future) that he was the third noble with the name Cornelius destined by fate for sovereignty in the capital—the first two having been Lucius Cornelius Cinna and Lucius Cornelius Sulla.[11] During the final days of November, he and his lieutenants in Rome secretly solicited the support of people who seemed "ripe for revolution by disposition or fortune," and thus increased the number of the conspiracy's adherents in accordance with the instructions of Catiline. The night of the *Saturnalia* festival (19 December) was selected for the urban sedition. All the plotters agreed upon this as a suitable date except Cethegus, who was impatient by nature and felt that it was too long of a delay; but since he was out-voted, he had to go along with it. In so far as the details of the uprising were concerned, it was decided that a large number of the citizenry as well as the nobility should be slaughtered; only the children of Pompey were to be spared for sure—they might be useful as hostages against the general's reprisals. Men supporting the conspiracy were assigned by lot to their various tasks: Some were to assist Cethegus in the massacre of senators; others were to help Gabinius in the general slaughter; some were to aid Cassius in setting fires; others were to stop up the aqueducts and kill people who tried to fetch water; still others were to plunder the treasury. In the meantime, torches and brimstone and arms were hidden at the house of Cethegus, whence they were to be distributed shortly before the urban sedition was initiated.[12]

Cicero knew that Lentulus was the chief conspiratorial leader within Rome, and he therefore diligently followed the praetor's actions through reports of his informers. Yet he was hampered by a lack of documentary proof on the guilt of the conspirators. Catiline was then an acknowledged enemy of the republic, but Cicero needed further evidence to prove that a "Trojan horse" was within the city walls. A chance of obtaining the necessary proof soon presented itself through the loyalty of some provincial subjects. While Lentulus was fine-tuning the conspiratorial machine, an opportunity arose which offered the possibility of adding great strength to the revolution. A northwestern province of the Roman Empire at that time was Gallia Transalpina (also known as Narbonensis after its capital Narbo) in the south of ancient Gaul. The Allobroges, a warlike Celtic tribe who resided in the northern part of this province where modern day Vienne is located, had of late incurred an overburdening amount of public and private debts on account of "the rapacity of the Roman officials." They had recently dispatched two ambassadors to Rome who were to present their complaints to the Senate. When the Senate failed to respond swiftly and helpfully to the entreaties of the Gallic legates, Lentulus decided to take advantage of their disgruntled dispositions. He realized that the chances of the conspiracy's success would certainly be increased by the support of a fierce Celtic tribe. Thus, he instructed Publius Umbrenus to sound out the Gauls on joining the rebellion. Umbrenus, one of the less important conspirators, knew the ambassadors personally from his business activities in their territory. He approached them with the suggestion that the ideal remedy for their adversity would be complicity in the daring *coup d'état* of Catiline. He introduced them to Gabinius, a key member of the inner circle of conspiratorial leaders, and enumerated the names of other important nobles who were supposedly supporting the plot. The envoys must have been impressed with the arguments of Umbrenus and Gabinius as they agreed to lend assistance to the rebellion. However, when the Gauls later had time to consider their decision with more care, they changed their minds. Weighing the severe consequences their people would suffer if the conspiracy failed against the possible rewards they would receive if they informed the official authorities of the plot, they decided to play it safe and remain loyal to the Roman state. They contacted the patron of their tribe at Rome, Quintus Fabius Sanga, and told him about the offer of the conspirators. He was a loyal citizen of the republic and a firm supporter of the establishment, and he therefore immediately notified Cicero of the situation.[13]

Cicero wisely judged that this was the opportunity he needed to obtain clear-cut, written evidence against the conspirators. So, he instructed the Gallic legates to play along with the plotters as if they were really intending to participate in the revolution. He asked them to request written documents about the conspiracy that were supposedly to be taken to their tribe but, in reality, were to be handed over to the consuls. The loyal Allobroges carried out the instructions of Cicero in masterful style. They arranged for Gabinius to introduce them to other members of the plotter's inner circle. They requested and obtained from these leaders written agreements which they claimed would be needed to induce their fellow tribesmen to take part in the revolt. Cassius even decided to proceed to Gaul himself in order to aid in rousing and directing the Celtic participation in the rebellion. He left immediately. Statilius and Gabinius took control of the arson teams which he had been directing in Rome. Lentulus persuaded Titus Volturcius, a friend of Gabinius and Caeparius, to accompany the Gallic ambassadors on their journey back to their province. Volturcius was to lead them first to Catiline so that they might confirm their agreement with the leader of the conspiracy himself. Lentulus entrusted Volturcius with a letter to Catiline suggesting that the rebel leader employ the help of all orders, "even the lowest." He also relayed a verbal message inquiring why Catiline was refusing to enlist the support of slaves and urging him to hasten his march on Rome.[14]

When Cicero was informed of these developments, he took prompt action to insure the capture of the damnatory letters. He contacted two brave and loyal praetors, Lucius Flaccus and Caius Pomptinus; he apprised them of the situation and instructed them on the action they should take. Volturcius and the Gallic envoys were intending to leave by way of the Mulvian Bridge to the north of Rome on the night of 2 December. Thus, on the designated evening, the praetors went with a special force of armed young men to lie in wait for them. As the party approached the bridge, a swift surprise attack was made upon them. Volturcius bravely drew his sword and called on his associates to fight, but as the Allobroges perceived what was happening, they quickly surrendered and turned the letters over to the praetors. Volturcius had no choice but to surrender as well. Early on the next morning, the praetors turned over the prisoners and letters to Cicero. With the apprehension of these witnesses and the messages they were conveying, the urban part of the Catilinarian Conspiracy was doomed, since Cicero thereafter possessed the documentary evidence that he needed to take decisive action against the seditious "Trojan horse" in the capital. On that momentous third day of December, the ceaseless vigilance of the consul was finally to attain fruition.[15]

Cicero summoned the *patres conscripti* to the Temple of Concord, between the Capitoline Hill and the Forum, and had the leaders of the sedition in Rome—Lentulus, Cethegus, Statilius, Gabinius, and Caeparius—arrested and escorted to the meeting under guard. While the senators were gathering, he also dispatched another trustworthy praetor, Caius Sulpicius, to search the house of Cethegus for the weapons that the Allobroges had disclosed were stockpiled there.

Cicero opened the session by introducing Volturcius. The latter was offered a pardon through the "good faith" of the Senate if he would reveal what he knew about the conspiracy. He was obviously not one of the inner circle, since he knew neither all the details of the plot nor all the members in it. He was merely a close friend and associate of Gabinius and was being used as a messenger. But he did know some of the conspirators and had knowledge of the general nature of the conspiracy. He identified Publius Autronius, Servius Sulla, and Lucius Vargunteius, among others, as being associated with the plot. He reported that Lentulus had forwarded a message to Catiline advising him to free and employ slaves in his march on the city—an appeal for another bloody slave war, which evoked memories of the wretched conflict a decade earlier against Spartacus. He also revealed that Catiline was requested to march toward Rome as soon as possible so that he might apprehend the citizens who would be fleeing from the fires and massacres therein. Next, the Allobroges were brought in and related how Lentulus, Cethegus, and Statilius had furnished them with letters for their fellow tribesmen. They divulged that Lucius Cassius and others had urged them to hasten to Italy as soon as possible to support the rebellion with their cavalry forces, and that Lentulus had assured them that the Sibylline Books had predicted that he was the third Cornelius destined to rule Rome. The conspirators were then forced to identify their seals on and handwriting in the letters apprehended by the praetors at the Mulvian Bridge. These epistles were read aloud to the Senate, and their contents confirmed the testimony given by Volturcius and the Gauls so that the plotters had no choice other than to confess to their treasonous scheming. The copious supply of new weapons that Sulpicius had discovered at the house of Cethegus and brought to the Senate also confirmed the patent guilt of the conspirators.

When all the damnatory evidence had been presented, Cicero requested that the senators proffer their opinions on the matter. The conspiratorial leaders were universally condemned, and several decrees were passed to deal with the situation. Cicero was given a vote of thanks in the highest terms of praise for his valor, prudence, and wisdom. A supplication was also decreed to the gods for their kindness in allowing the consul "to save the city from conflagration, the citizens from massacre, and Italy from war"—an exceedingly impressive honor since Cicero was the first Roman magistrate ever to receive such a *supplicatio* in a non-military capacity. Praises were also imparted to the praetors Flaccus and Pomptinus and to the other consul Antonius for their assistance in opposing the conspiracy. Lentulus was forced to resign his praetorship and defrocked of his purple-bordered senatorial toga for the second time in his checkered career. He and the other conspiratorial leaders were then placed in the custody of certain senators until their punishment could be determined.[16]

As evening arrived, Cicero adjourned the Senate and went out to the multitude of citizens who were eagerly awaiting information on what had happened. The triumphant consul then delivered another *contio* to the people assembled in the Forum—his famous *Third Oration Against Catiline* in which he vividly recounted how he had uncovered and forestalled the dangerous conspiracy of Catiline's henchmen, which would have wreaked havoc upon the city. A reversal in public opinion swiftly took place thereafter. Cicero was praised to the skies for saving the possessions of the wealthy from plunder, the homes of the poor from fire, and the republic from an attack by the Gauls. The designs of Catiline, which earlier had been looked upon favorably by a good portion of the masses, were now cursed. The urban mob was not averse to civil upheavals, which might provide opportunities for plunder; but an incendiary conflagration seemed very "cruel, monstrous, and especially calamitous to themselves since their sole possessions were the daily food they ate and the dirty clothes they wore."[17]

The populace triumphantly escorted Cicero to the house of a friend where he was going to spend the night, as a religious ceremony was being conducted at his own home by his wife Terentia and the Vestal Virgins in honor of the *Bona Dea* (Good Goddess). He whiled away the night pondering what kind of punishment should be inflicted upon the conspiratorial leaders. He was hesitant to employ the death penalty because of the precarious legality of such an act. The old Porcian and Sempronian laws provided Roman citizens condemned to capital punishment with protection from hasty death sentences; however, time was of the utmost importance with Catiline preparing to march on Rome.

A strange portent supposedly occurred during the night that strengthened the consul's determination to act forcefully against the conspirators. Plutarch reported in his *Life of Cicero* that just as he was contemplating severe action, a lustrous flame burst forth from the dying embers on the altar at his home. The holy maidens interpreted this to signify that the Good Goddess approved of the course on which the consul was meditating. They directed Cicero's wife Terentia to go to her husband and encourage him "to execute what he had resolved for the good of his country since the goddess had sent a great light to increase his safety and glory." Terentia hurried to Cicero and related to him what had happened. She, his brother Quintus, and his philosophical companion Publius Nigidius all incited his determination to take severe action against the dangerous traitors.[18]

The following day witnessed the airing of fraudulent testimony in the Senate and an attempted rescue of the captive conspirators. One of the less important members of the conspiracy, Lucius Tarquinius, proffered an accusation that Crassus was privy to the plot. This seemed to be an incredible charge as Crassus himself had given Cicero the evidence necessary to obtain the *senatus consultum ultimum* of 21 October. The senators—many of whom were friends with and indebted to the great financier—were very outraged at such an obvious falsehood, and they decreed that Tarquinius was a liar and that his testimony should not be accepted. It is quite possible that Cicero may have put Tarquinius up to such an accusation against the influential *popularis*. Crassus felt that this was the case and subsequently held a grudge against the wily orator. Cicero knew that Crassus had an unhealthy habit of coming forward in defense of bad characters (e.g., after the "Pisonian Conspiracy") and thus may have been trying to place Crassus in such a position that he would not feel safe to do the same in this dangerous situation. It would therefore be much easier for Cicero to argue that severe measures must be used against the captive plotters.

The optimate leaders Quintus Catulus and Gaius Piso strove to arouse similar suspicions against Caesar. Both were motivated by partisan politics and personal revenge: Caesar had defeated Catulus in the race for the prestigious office of *pontifex maximus* and had prosecuted Piso in an extortion trial. Failing to obtain a believable accuser, they spread rumors across the city about the complicity of Caesar in the conspiracy. The facts that Caesar was then the chief priest of the state and had been elected to a praetorship for the year 62 were all the more reasons for him to be disinclined to jeopardize his position by involvement in the desperate designs of Catiline. Caesar was no more complicit in the conspiracy than was his wealthy associate; and the efforts of Catulus and Piso achieved little else than to incite some hotheaded equestrian youths to threaten the popular leader with swords a couple of days later. When these partisan squabbles were completed, the Senate voted to reward Volturcius and the Allobroges for the information that they had given on the previous day.[19]

While the senators were occupied with these matters, the dependents of Lentulus and Cethegus were attempting to rescue the captive conspirators, but with little success. Fortunately, Cicero was made cognizant of these activities in time and strengthened the guards around the houses where the culprits were being held. He also directed the praetors "to administer the oath of enlistment to the populace" so that a citizen militia would be available to meet any emergencies with force. The supposed portent of the *Bona Dea* and the possibility of the plotters escaping convinced Cicero of the necessity for decisive action. Thus, he summoned the Senate to meet on the following morning.[20]

On 5 December in 63 BC, the senators came together prepared to offer their *sententiae* (opinions) on what punishments seemed fitting for the dangerous conspirators whose guilt of treasonable conduct had already been proved. Cicero requested that the consul-elect Silanus open the discussion with his views. The latter advanced the opinion that the conspirators already in confinement and those subsequently apprehended should receive the death penalty. The majority of the senior senators who were polled thereafter agreed with this judgment until the praetor-elect Julius Caesar offered his opinion. Caesar spoke as a wise and cautious statesman, and he urged that moderation be employed lest an unhealthy precedent be established that might be misused on the innocent in the future. Just as he had done in the Rabirian trial, he again presented himself as the defender of the rights of the citizen from oppressive action on the part of the senatorial oligarchy. Caesar suggested that their minds were clouded by hatred and fear, and that in such a climate it was difficult to employ sound judgment. He intimated that a harsh and hasty punishment might later cause a reaction in public feeling against them for illegal treatment of Roman citizens. He then coolly proposed a punishment certainly more unprecedented than that proffered by Silanus: that the possessions of the condemned be confiscated, that they be imprisoned for life in various towns throughout Italy, that these towns be considered enemies of Rome if their prisoners were allowed to escape, and that any alleviation of the sentences of the condemned be prohibited by law.

The speech of Caesar had a marked effect upon the senators. Those who followed adopted his proposal, and many who had spoken before altered their opinions in favor of Caesar's because it seemed more advantageous for Cicero who might be "less subject to censure if he did not put the conspirators to death." Cicero perceived that the sentiment of the Senate was swaying and rose to inject his own opinion into the debate. In this *Fourth*

Oration Against Catiline, Cicero urged that the senators place the welfare of the republic, its citizens, and themselves before that of their consul. He selflessly exhorted them to vote for a just penalty and not to worry about his security or reputation because he was willing to bear any danger and misfortune as long as the safety and dignity of the Senate and Roman people were preserved. He condemned the schemes of the conspirators, and after discussing the merits of the two chief opinions (i.e., those of Silanus and of Caesar), he suggested that the latter's "proposition seems to have in it injustice if commanded, and difficulty if requested." Nevertheless, he went on to say that he was prepared to carry out whatever sentence upon which the Senate might agree.

The former consul Catulus then threw his support behind the death penalty. Yet many of the senators were still undecided when the tribune-elect Marcus Cato received his turn to speak. Although still a young man, he had gained the respect of many of his colleagues because of the purity of his personal life, the uprightness of his character, and the sincerity of his convictions. Cato reasoned that the Senate was no longer dealing with wayward citizens but with mortal enemies (*hostes*) who threatened their liberty, their property, their constitution, and their very lives. He argued that it was not the time for clemency or compassion when so many things of great value were at stake. He posited that their decision would probably have a great effect upon the rebel armies, prophesying that if they acted sternly and energetically, the courage of Catiline's followers would no doubt be shaken. The senators were so greatly swayed by the righteous vigor, unadorned eloquence, and common sense of Cato's oration that they almost unanimously "changed to the support of his motion and voted for the imposition of the death penalty upon the conspirators." With the moral support of the Senate behind him, Cicero decided to carry out the executions immediately. He must have felt that this was necessary to prevent the possibility of another rescue attempt by some of the conspirators still at large.[21]

Upon leaving the senatorial meeting, Cicero instructed the three urban magistrates in charge of the state prison to ready the execution chamber. After posting guards along the *Via Sacra* (Sacred Way) that led through the Forum to the prison, he proceeded to the house on the Palatine Hill where the chief conspirator was being confined. With a strong guard at his heels and the awed populace looking on, Cicero personally escorted Lentulus back down the Sacred Way to the jail; the praetors brought the four other captives in similar fashion. Inside the prison complex, twelve feet below the upper level, was a little chamber known as the *Tullianum*. It was in this dark and foul pit that the public executioner performed his wretched duties. One by one the five condemned plotters were lowered into this hideous hole to meet their fate—strangulation. As Cicero emerged from the jail, he laconically announced to the multitude gathered outside: *Vixerunt* ("They have lived")—a sardonic way of signifying that they were now dead. Then, accompanied by Rome's leading nobles, he triumphantly walked through the crowds toward his home. *Optimates, populares, equites,* and the common people all alike openly acknowledged how greatly indebted they were to the eloquent consul for delivering them from such a serious and imminent danger. All along his way home he was greeted by the applause and acclamation of the multitudes who wished to salute him and by curious women peering from their housetops, anxious to gaze upon the man who was being hailed as "the savior and founder of his country."[22]

Within the next few days, other citizens who were implicated in the conspiracy were rounded up and questioned by the Senate. As there was no unequivocal evidence available against these individuals, nothing more severe than public condemnation or suspension from office could be decreed. Yet this official leniency was not observed by some of Rome's noble *patres.* Under the ancient Roman tradition of unlimited paternal authority (*patria potestas*), several aristocratic fathers had errant sons that were supporting Catiline put to death. Thus, the central goal of the Catiline's conspiracy—obtaining control of Rome—had been foiled. The diligent action and brilliant oratory of the consul Cicero had effectively broken up the urban sedition and unified virtually all elements of the Roman citizen body behind the government. With Rome securely under the control of Cicero's conservative coalition, the rest of conspiratorial plot had little hope of success.

Concurrent with the government's success in Rome, its agents were obstructing conspiratorial actions on the peninsula. Catiline had dispatched his own assistants to various parts of Italy in hopes of gaining support for his revolutionary designs. He and Manlius had succeeded in raising an army of some 20,000 troops and taking effective control of Etruria to the northwest of Rome, but the other conspiratorial envoys had not fared so well. They had succeeded in staging a series of outbreaks in late November and early December, but these uprisings had been ill-conceived, rashly begun, and feebly supported. The disturbances in Apulia and Bruttium in the south were of little account and had easily been quashed by government officials. Those in the Picene and Gallic districts in the east and north were more serious and had wider backing; but they too had been overcome. Metellus Celer had arrested, tried, and imprisoned the supporters of the rebellion in Picenum, and Gaius Murena had done the same in lower Gaul (the firebrand Cassius may have been among those sentenced to rot in a Gallic prison).[23]

Such effective action on the part of the republican government must have greatly disheartened Catiline and his rebel followers in Etruria. But as long as they did not know of the victory of Cicero at Rome, they still had hopes for the ultimate success of their movement. If Lentulus, Cethegus, and the revolutionary leaders could gain control of the capital along with his stronghold in Etruria, Catiline hoped that the other discontented peoples on the peninsula might be inspired to rally to his banner. He had a considerable force around Faesulae, but only about a quarter of these men were properly armed. From this fact it seems safe to assume that the majority of his supporters were the dispossessed or debtor farmers who inhabited the region. They were backing Catiline's revolutionary schemes in hopes of obtaining debt cancellation, new debt laws, and more land when the "new order" was established. As long as Catiline had a chance of success, they could be counted on; but when defeat loomed, their loyalty might revert to the government and more peaceful means of protest as Cato had predicted. The hard core of Catiline's army was composed of the Sullan veterans in Etruria and the discontented and ruined members of the radical *populares* from Rome. The former were deeply in debt and had failed to make it as farmers. They were looking back longingly to the days of glory and plunder during the civil strife of the Sullan Era. The latter were hopelessly in debt like Catiline, and they had little or no chance to rise in the *cursus honorum*. They were anathema to the ruling *optimates* and had neither the following nor the monetary resources of other *populares* such as Crassus and Caesar. These two groups could be counted on to stand by Catiline in good or bad times. The latter soon arrived, for when the report of Cicero's victory in the capital reached the rebel forces, the timid majority took flight and swiftly dispersed. With only a few thousand hardcore supporters left and his hope of seizing Rome smashed, Catiline reasoned that the only sensible move left was retreat to Gaul.

Therefore, he led his loyal troops toward a pass in the Apennine Mountains just north of Pistoria (modern Pistoia). But when he arrived there, he found out that Metellus Celer was waiting at the foot of the pass to block his descent. Metellus had just learned of Catiline's intentions, and he had accordingly made a forced march from Picenum in order to intercept the conspirator's retreat. To add further discomfiture to this adverse situation, the troops of the consul Antonius were fast approaching Catiline's rear. The rebel force was thus hemmed in by Metellus on the route up to Gaul and by Antonius on the road back towards Rome. Catiline could surrender or fight. The former meant certain death, but even if it had not, there would have been no thought of surrender on Catiline's part. Such a word was foreign to the vocabulary of that proud, ruthless, and audacious man. He had to fight. The only question was with whom, Metellus or Antonius? He chose Antonius, even though this meant turning his back on Gaul and risking battle with a larger force. The Greek historian Cassius Dio suggested that Catiline was hoping that his old friend and former running mate would allow himself to be beaten by the rebel forces. From what is known of Catiline's character, it seems more likely that he would have been motivated by revenge rather than the cowardly hope of escape through a false victory. He certainly could not have appreciated the fact that Antonius had turned away from their friendship and made a deal to support his political rival Cicero. In any case, his decision fell upon the consular army to the south.

Catiline assembled his troops in the mountains above Pistoria and addressed them courageously. Sallust reported that he summoned all of the eloquence he possessed, and he exhorted his men to fight bravely and remember their past valor as everything they had dreamed of was at stake—glory, honor, wealth, liberty, the future of their country, and their very lives. He then led his army in battle formation down to a small but level plain in the hills and sent away all their horses. There would be no retreat; it was going to be a fight to the finish, and everyone knew it. The government forces were also making ready for battle—but not with Antonius at their head. He complained of illness and passed off the command to his chief lieutenant Marcus Petreius. There is no way to know for sure why Antonius declined to lead his troops into battle. He could have been fearful of facing the vicious Catiline in open combat. Maybe he had no stomach for fighting against a former friend and fellow noble. Or perhaps he was ill on the day of the confrontation. In any case, his withdrawal had little effect upon the outcome of the battle. Marcus Petreius was a thirty-year veteran of the Roman legions. He knew most of the men in the ranks and was an able commander. Sallust reported that he too exhorted his soldiers to bravery prior to the fight. He spoke with contempt for the opposing forces, calling them no more than a band of brigands. He raised the spirits of his men to a fighting pitch by reminding them that their country, families, altars, and hearths were at stake.

On a morning in January of the year 62, the trumpets sounded and the battle commenced. The sanguinary struggle was fierce and desperate to the end with a good part of the long battle occurring at close quarters and with short swords. Not a man in Catiline's army survived, and many of the best fighters in the opposing army were either killed or seriously wounded. Catiline himself fought harder than anyone on the field, advancing farther into the enemy lines than any of his fellow soldiers. In so dying, he exhibited the bravery with which he had been able to attract the respect of so many followers. As the Roman historian Lucius Florus aptly commented: *pulcherrima morte, si pro patria sic concidisset* ("a most glorious death, if only he had fallen thus in the service of his country").[24]

The news of the victory near Pistoria was greeted in Rome with mixed emotions: with happiness and relief that the government forces had triumphed and ended the threat of Catiline's rebellion, but also with regret and grief for the loss of lives encountered in the battle. However, there was consolation in the fact that it could have been much worse if Cicero had not foiled the urban phase of the plot. Catiline met his death within a month after Cicero had executed the urban conspiratorial leaders. Cicero therefore finished his consulship at the peak of his political power and popularity. He was even hailed as *pater patriae* ("the father of his country") by an official vote of the Tribal Assembly just after he left office. He was the first Roman to be honored in this manner—an honor that he well deserved for saving the Roman Republic from the Catilinarian Conspiracy.[25]

ALPS

Po R.

GALLIA CISALPINA

APENNINE MOUNTAINS
Pistoria ×
· Faesulae
Arno R.
· Arretium
ETRURIA
· Camerino
Tiber R.   PICENUM

CORSICA

Rome).   .Praeneste
LATIUM Arpinum
CAMPANIA

· Naples   APULIA

SARDINIA

BRUTTIUM

SICILIA

AFRICA

MAJOR REGIONS
· Important Cities
× Battle Site

Ill. 12: Map of Italy
in the Ciceronian Era

Illustration 12   Map of Italy in the Ciceronian Era.

VII The Aftermath and Modern Echoes

"It is this spirit which has commonly ruined great nations when one party desires to triumph over another by any and every means."

Sallust, *Bellum Iugurthinum* 42. 4

Even if Cicero had not succeeded in thwarting the deleterious designs of Catiline, a victory for the conspiratorial forces probably would have been only a temporary one. Pompey the Great, backed by the resources of the Roman Empire, undoubtedly would have returned at the head of his loyal legions and mercilessly crushed the radical regime of Catiline in a civil war. This probably would have resulted in a Pompeian military dictatorship—something which few citizens of the republic could have looked forward to with favor. In fact, the threat of just such a development aided Cicero in bringing to the support of the government what he called the *coniunctio bonorum omnium*. By leading this "union of all good men" to victory over the desperate schemes of the conspirators, Cicero thwarted any designs that Pompey might have had of marching on Rome with his armies. By foiling Catiline's conspiracy, and thus preventing a massive civil war, Cicero saved his fellow citizens from needless bloodshed, added a few years of life to the republican constitution, and rightfully earned the thanks and praise bestowed upon him. Nevertheless, the consul's political accomplishment was likewise only temporary. As soon as the dangers had passed with Catiline's military defeat and Pompey's peaceful return, Cicero's *coniunctio* splintered upon the renewed factional strife of the *optimates* and the *populares*. The haggard republic would only see a short period of that *otium cum dignitate* ("peace with honor") for which its diligent consul had hoped and worked.

The short-term result of the failure of the conspiracy was a strengthening of the position and prestige of the optimate faction within the senatorial oligarchy. Most of its members had looked askance upon the seditious Catiline all along, while many of the popular leaders had backed the prodigal patrician in his early bids for power; and some were under suspicion of being privy to his conspiratorial designs. Catiline had openly styled himself as "a friend of the people" and had appealed to the same discontented elements of the Roman citizen body that Crassus and Caesar were courting. As a result, the *populares* were temporarily stained with a stigma of revolution while the *optimates* emerged from the episode with a patina of patriotism. However, the resurgent *optimates* soon lost this advantage. They foolishly abused their precarious power and thereby set the stage for a revival of the *populares* under a much more talented and inspired leader. Upon the return of Pompey, the optimate faction was intent on demeaning the popular general and exercising oligarchic power. Pompey was allowed to celebrate magnificent triumphs for his Mediterranean campaigns against the pirates and his Near East victories over Mithridates and Seleucid Syria; but the senators then torturously debated the Eastern treaties of the general and land grants for his soldiers, and they tediously delayed a decision on an appeal from Crassus and the equestrians to lower their overly optimistic and high bids on tribute collecting from the new Eastern provinces—humiliating the proud general and embarrassing the great financier for over two years. Cicero, the wise elder statesman with friends in both factions, tried to mediate the stalemate by counseling moderation and compromise and by transforming his *coniunctio bonorum* into a *concordia ordinum* ("a concord of the orders"). But his words of wisdom fell upon the deaf ears of jealous oligarchs and ambitious dynasts.

The long-term result of the failure of the conspiracy was a strengthening of the position and power of Julius Caesar at the head of a revived popular faction. Having served effectively as a praetor and high priest in Rome and then having gained military glory as a governor in Spain during the factional squabbling in the years after Cicero's consulship (62–61 BC), he came back to Rome determined to unite the dispirited *populares* and run for the consulship (60). As he had supported both Pompey and Crassus in his earlier career, he was able to curb their feuding and bring them and their resources together to back his run for the highest office in the state. The First Triumvirate of Caesar, Crassus, and Pompey—backed by the urban masses, the equestrian publicans, and loyal legions—was able to out-vote the senatorial oligarchy, dominate the politics of Rome, and control the provinces of the empire for the next decade. Caesar won his consulship (59), repaid his political partners by getting what they wanted in bills from the Tribal Assembly, and then completed a spectacular proconsulship in which he conquered all of *Gallia Comata* in the west (58–50 BC). He added three new provinces to the empire—Gallia Belgica, Narbonensis, and Aquitania—and gained as much wealth as Crassus and more glory than Pompey. With the death of Crassus in an eastern campaign with the Parthians and the return of Pompey to the optimate faction in the late 50s, a civil war between Caesar and the *populares* and Pompey and the *optimates* was inevitable. Caesar was the better general and defeated his rival to become *Dictator Reipublicae* (49–44 BC). The defeat of Catiline's plots in the 60s gave Caesar time to mature as a politician and to develop as a general. Thus, by saving the republic from the *coniuratio* of Catiline, Cicero preserved it for the later *dominatio* of Caesar—and the efficient autocracy of Caesar was a better outcome than a vicious tyranny of Catiline or an inept dictatorship of Pompey.

As a hero of the republic and a leading statesman in the Senate, Cicero was asked to join or support the Triumvirate. His reverence for the republican constitution prevented him from doing so, and in revenge the triumvirs allowed the *popularis* tribune Clodius to pass a bill in the assembly outlawing anyone who put a citizen to death without a trial—an action which Cicero had committed as consul against five of the urban conspirators. He went into voluntary exile for eighteen months to Thessalonica in Greece (58–57 BC). However, his wide connections in the Senate, his broad popularity among the people in Rome and Italy, and his friendship with Pompey soon resulted in his triumphant return. Yet, he could not help but be dispirited by the gradual destruction of the free republic—first by Cato and the obstructionist oligarchy, then by the popular triumvirs, again by the rising factional violence in the streets of Rome, and finally by the civil war and Caesar's dictatorship. So, he spent much of the late 50s and early 40s in retirement from active politics, and he only occasionally gave senatorial speeches, made court appearances, and served as the proconsular governor of Cilicia in southern Asia Minor for a year (51–50 BC). During most of these years, Cicero resided in his various Italian homes and villas and became the most prolific and eloquent author in the Latin language. His good friend and confidant in the equestrian business class Titus Atticus oversaw the publication and distribution of his voluminous works. His Verrine orations, his Catilinarian invectives, his court speeches, and his philosophical writings made him the leading *literatus* of the day and elevated Latin letters to near equality with Greek literature. Among his works on political philosophy, Cicero left posterity his thoughts on the ethical principles and the public responsibilities of politicians in his *De Officiis* and his recommendations on how the ideal republic should be structured and governed in the *De Re Publica*. Caesar much respected Cicero as a man of letters and occasionally enjoyed his company for dinners and discussions. That may be why the optimate politicians who had survived the civil war did not include Cicero in the plot to assassinate the dictator on 15 March 44 BC. By this time Cicero had outlived all of the greatest politicians of his day and had become the most famous statesman of the age. He was called upon to save the republic again, and he led a senatorial coalition that kept the heirs of Caesar divided and at bay for over a year. But when Octavian Caesar, Marcus Antonius, and Marcus Lepidus came together in a Second Triumvirate and determined to take revenge upon Caesar's assassins and the remnant of the *optimates*, Cicero lost his life in their vicious proscription in December of 43—twenty years after he had saved the republic from the Catilinarian Conspiracy. Through the next dozen years, the Caesarians fought amongst themselves for control of the Roman world with Octavian winning out as the last faction leader and politician-general of the "Roman Revolution" (43–31 BC). He finally ended the political strife of the last century, but as Caesar Augustus transformed the Roman state from a republic to an autocracy as the *princeps* (first man) and *imperator* (emperor) of imperial Rome (27). Sallust, a younger contemporary of Cicero who had been a *popularis* politician and had served as a general, governor, and official under Caesar, was appalled at the murders of Caesar and Cicero and by the endemic violence of republican politics. Rather than serve under the triumvirs, he followed Cicero's example and retired from public life to his beautiful villa outside of Rome, and he took up historical research and writing in the late 40s and early 30s—with the goal of elucidating the problems which were destroying the republic. His partially extant *Historiae* and his more famous monographs on the *Bellum Iugurthinum* and the *Bellum Catilinae* were the results of his efforts. The public careers and literary works of Cicero and Sallust illuminated the chaotic political climate of the late Roman Republic, and they offer somber warnings to the citizens of modern republics and parliamentary democracies because so many of the events they witnessed and the phenomena they described seem to have modern echoes.[1]

Ancient philosophers and historians praised the concept of the mixed constitution with checks and balances between the elements of monarchy, aristocracy, and democracy, and they extolled the Romans for creating such an exemplary commonwealth in their republic. However, perfectly conceived constitutions are still piloted by imperfect human beings who are not always inspired by the best of motives. This case study of the Ciceronian Era has revealed how the overweening desire for power and lust for wealth in the governing classes at Rome led to competing factions in the Senate, divisive politics in the Forum, and military revolutions in the field that ultimately resulted in the demise of the free republic and the emergence of an imperial autocracy. The founding fathers of the modern republics in Europe and the Americas based upon the Roman model attempted to fine-tune their creations—even adopting some of Cicero's suggestions for maintaining better stability in their constitutions and governments. Yet, two and a quarter centuries into our modern experiments, some of the same deleterious trends that led the Roman Republic down the road to ruin are rampant in our modern commonwealths: divisive and extremist political factions competing fiercely for the spoils of power; the ponderous and corrosive power of money and its influence in election campaigns and policy decisions; the vicious "politics of personal destruction" in political advertising; the use of the courts for political prosecutions; and in some cases (particularly in Latin America), military involvement in civil institutions. And electronic technology has allowed the modern players of divisive politics to spread their factional propaganda and vicious rumors faster and farther than Cicero or Catiline could have dreamed of in their day. Thucydides in classical Greece and Sallust in republican Rome both commented on how the leaders of the divisive political groups of their chaotic times employed specious pretexts and patriotic phrases, claiming either to be protecting the rights of the people or to be defending the authority of the state, but in reality were just fighting to get control of the reins of power for their own aggrandizement. Human nature and political practice seem to have changed little, if at all, from ancient history to modern times. Sallust wisely commented "It is this spirit which has commonly ruined great nations when one party desires to triumph over another by any and every means." Whether the wiser statesmen and citizens of modern republics can overcome the divisive forces at work in modern politics, follow Cicero's adage *cedant arma togae* ("let arms yield to the toga"), and save their states from the fate of Rome remains to be seen.[2]

Notes

NOTES TO CHAPTER I

1. This account of Catiline's nocturnal gathering on 6 November 63 BC is based upon data from Cicero, *Oratio in Catilinam* I. 4; Sallust, *Bellum Catilinae* 27–28; Florus, *Epitomae de Tito Livio Bellorum Omnium Annorum DCC* II. 12; Appian, *Bella Civilia* II. 2–3; Dio, *Historia Romana* XXXVII. 32–33; and Plutarch, *Cicero* 16. For the narrative context and specific details, see Ch. V of this book.
2. For the sake of readers new to the field of late republican studies, I have used slightly longer abbreviations for the ancient sources listed in the endnotes than is customary in scholarly tomes. The full titles of the Latin and Greek texts of the ancient works (with accessible English translations) employed in the writing of this book are contained in the "Ancient Sources" section of the bibliography, while classic and recent works of modern scholarship used in the research for it are found in the "Modern Scholarship" section.

NOTES TO CHAPTER II

1. Ancient narrative histories covering the early phases of the "Roman Revolution" from ca. 133–67 BC include Velleius Paterculus, *Historiae Romanae* II. 1–33; Florus, *Epitomae* II. 1–11; Appian, *Bella Civilia* I. 1–14; and Dio, *Historia Romana* XII–XXXV, with Sallust's *Bellum Iugurthinum* providing a case study therein. Standard modern works on the late republic and its political problems include R. E. Smith, *The Failure of the Roman Republic* (Cambridge, 1955); Frank Burr Marsh, *A History of the Roman World*, 3rd ed. (London, 1963); Lily Ross Taylor, *Party Politics in the Age of Caesar* (Berkeley, 1964); Stewart Perowne, *Death of the Roman Republic* (Garden City, NY, 1968); Erich S. Gruen, *The Last Generation of the Roman Republic* (Berkeley, 1974); H. H. Scullard, *From the Gracchi to Nero*, 5th ed. (London, 1982); and P. A. Brunt, *The Fall of the Roman Republic and Related Essays* (Oxford, 1988). More recent works include those by A. J. Langguth, *A Noise of War* (New York, 1994); Tom Holland, *Rubicon: The Last Years of the Roman Republic* (New York, 2003); David Shotter, *The Fall of the Roman Republic*, 2nd ed. (London, 2005); and Edward Bispham, *The Roman Republic: 264–44 BC* (London, 2009).
2. Sall., *Bellum Iug.* 41 and *Bellum Cat.* 10. 3; the shortened version of the latter providing the cliché "money is the root of all evil."
3. Cic., *Oratio pro Sestio* 45. 96. *Populares* is the plural of the Latin word *popularis*, which means "popular," "agreeable to the people," "of or relating

to the people" (as opposed to the aristocracy), "democratic"; hence, the plural *populares* refers to the "popular faction" or the "friends of the people." *Optimates* is the plural of the Latin word *optimas*, which means "one of the best," "aristocratic"; hence, the plural *optimates* refers to "the aristocrats" or the "oligarchic faction."

4. There has been a long debate among modern scholars over the definition and place of factions in the political life of the late republic; late nineteenth- and early twentieth-century historians like Mommsen and Münzer employed language which compared them too closely to the conservative and liberal parliamentary "parties" of modern Europe, and late twentieth-century historians like Gruun and Brunt used language which dismissed their existence very nearly to ephemeral "political alliances" or "shifting combinations" of senatorial politicians in times of crisis. In between these extreme positions are found the views of mid-twentieth century classicists and historians like Taylor and Scullard, who saw them as *partes* or *factiones* in the ancient sense of those terms which allowed republican politicians to ally with each other in political "coalitions" and through family connections based upon adherence to pro-senatorial and conservative stances or to anti-senatorial and populist programs. As Cicero and Sallust, the best ancient contemporary sources for the period under study, regularly used the terms *optimates* and *populares* and described their members and programs in their writings, I have followed a middle position in this work that distinguishes the differences between the ancient factions and modern parties but recognizes their existence as coalitions within the political framework of the time. For some of the key modern scholarship on this debate, see Theodore Mommsen, *Römische Geschichte*, vol. 3 (1856) = *The History of Rome: A New Edition* by Dero A. Saunders and John H. Collins (New York, 1958), pp. 8–9, 24ff.; F. Münzer, *Römische Adelsparteien und Adelsfamilien* (Stuttgart, 1920), pp. 283–373; Roland Syme, *The Roman Revolution* (Oxford, 1939), pp. 10–27; Lily Ross Taylor, *Party Politics*, pp. 6–15; Scullard, *From the Gracchi to Nero*, pp. 6–7; Gruun, *Last Generation*, pp. 47–82; Brunt, *Fall of the Roman Republic*, pp. 443–502; and Anthony Everitt, *Cicero: The Life and Times of Rome's Greatest Politician* (New York, 2001), p. 14 and *passim*.

5. Sall., *Bellum Iug.* 63. 6 and *Bellum Cat.* 20. 7–8, respectively.

6. Sall., *Bellum Cat.* 20. 8.

7. Sall., *Bellum Cat.* 38. 2.

8. Sall., *Bellum Cat.* 38. 3.

9. Taylor, *Party Politics*, p. 13; *cf.* Syme, *Roman Revolution,* pp. 10–27; Scullard, *From the Gracchi to Nero*, pp. 5–7; and Brunt, *Fall of the Roman Republic*, p. 502.

10. Edward Spenser Beesly, *Catiline, Clodius and Tiberius* (London, 1878), p. 5. Though a socialist writing at the height of the British Empire in the nineteenth century, Beesly seems to have understood the temper of late republican politics well.

11. *Equites* is the plural of the Latin word *eques*, which means "a horseman" or "a knight"; the *equites* were a distinct order in the Roman commonwealth between the aristocratic senatorial order above, and the common farmers and tradesmen below. Their title was a holdover from the early republic, when the census takers determined from the material resources of the citizen body which families were able to field a fully armed cavalryman. Those families beneath the senatorial order who could do so were enrolled in the equestrian order. The famous Augustan Era poet Ovid was the one who expressed his aversion to political life in *Tristia* IV. 10. 33–38.

12. Beesly, *Catiline*, p. 7; *cf*. P. A. Brunt, "The *Equites* in the Late Republic," *Second International Conference of Economic History*, 1962 (Paris, 1965), vol. 1, pp. 117–37; and Scullard, *From the Gracchi to Nero*, pp. 8–9.
13. The term *latifundia* comes from the Latin words *latus* and *fundus* and means "large landed estate." For the Italian countryside and farming, see T.W. Potter, *Roman Italy* (Berkeley, 1987), pp. 94–124.
14. Quotations respectively from Sall., *Bellum Iug.* 41. 8; and P. A. Brunt, "The Conspiracy of Catiline," *History Today*, vol. 13 (1962), p. 1; *cf*. Appian, *Bella Civ.* I. 7.
15. Sall., *Bellum Cat.* 33. 1. For a discussion of the harsh treatment given to Roman farmers who failed to pay their debts, see Sir John Edwin Sandys, *A Companion to Latin Studies* (London, 1963), p. 309; and for descriptions of the adverse economic and social conditions which nurtured Catiline's conspiracy, consult R. von Pöhlmann, *Geschichte der sozialen Frage und des Sozialismus in der antiken Welt*, 3rd ed. (Munich, 1925), vol. 2, esp. pp. 352ff., 375ff., 429ff.; and Scullard, *From the Gracchi to Nero*, pp. 18–21.
16. *Capite censi* is Latin for "those counted by the head." As members of the landless urban mob, they had no landed possessions by which citizenship status was tabulated in the state censuses; thus, they were "counted by the head" alone. See Cic., *Oratio pro Murena* 24 for a description of the street gangs at elections, and Sall., *Bellum Iug.* 86. 3 for the quotation on seeking supporters among the poor. For modern comments, consult Taylor, *Party Politics*, pp. 41–47; Scullard, *From the Gracchi to Nero*, pp. 48–60; Gruun, *Last Generation*, pp. 433–48; Brunt, *Fall of the Roman Republic*, pp. 424–38; and Fergus Millar, *The Crowd in Rome in the Late Republic* (Ann Arbor, MI, 1998).
17. Sall., *Bellum Iug.* 86. 2–3.
18. Taylor, *Party Politics*, p. 47; *cf*. Scullard, *From the Gracchi to Nero*, pp. 48–60.
19. The pithy phrase used by Vell., *Hist. Rom.* II. 40. 4 to describe the jealously felt by other senatorial aristocrats toward the fame of Pompey.
20. The ancient narrative histories of Velleius, Florus, Appian, and Dio cited in note 1 of this chapter; and Plutarch's biographies of *Marius, Sulla*, and *Pompey* covered the careers of the politician-generals of the early first century. For useful modern works on this, see: Richard Evans, *Gaius Marius: A Political Biography* (Pretoria, 1994); Arthur Keaveny, *Sulla: The Last Republican*, 2nd ed. (London, 2005); Peter Greenhalgh, *Pompey: The Roman Alexander* (London, 1980); and R. J. Seager, *Pompey the Great, A Political Biography*, 2nd ed. (Oxford, 2002). For the constitutional framework in which they worked, see Andrew Lintott, *The Constitution of the Roman Republic* (Oxford, 1999).

NOTES TO CHAPTER III

1. The ancient sources which provided the most information on Catiline and his allies among the *populares* between 66 and 64 BC were Sallust's *Bellum Catilinae*; Asconius' *Enarratio ad Orationem in Toga Candida*; Cicero's *Orationes in Catilinam* I and II and various later court speeches; Appian's *Bella Civilia* II; Dio's *Historia Romana* XXXVI and XXXVII; Plutarch's biographies of *Cicero, Crassus*, and *Caesar*; and Suetonius' *Divus Julius*. Modern works on Catiline include: E. S. Beesly, *Catiline, Clodius and Tiberius* (London, 1878); Gaston Boissier, *La conjuration de Catilina* (Paris, 1905); E. G. Hardy, *The Catilinarian Conspiracy in Its Context: A Re-Study of the Evidence* (Oxford, 1924); A. Kaplan, *Catiline: The Man and His Role in the Roman Revolution*

(New York, 1968); Charles Matson Odahl, *The Catilinarian Conspiracy* (New Haven, 1971); and Victoria Emma Pagán, *Conspiracy Narratives in Roman History* (Austin, 2004).

2. Cic., *Oratio pro Caelio* 4. 10; Sall., *Bellum Cat.* 18. 2; Ascon., *Enarratio in Tog. Cand.* 75 and 79; Dio, *Hist. Rom.* XXXVI. 44. 3; Plut., *Crassus* 13 and *Caesar* 5; and Suet., *Div. Jul.* 9.

3. Quintus Cicero, *Commentariolum Petitionis Consulatus* 9; Ascon., *Enarratio in Tog. Cand.* 75; Florus, *Epit.* II. 12. 3; and Appian, *Bella Civ.* II. 1. 2.

4. Cic., *Oratio in Cat.* I. 6. 14 and *Oratio in Cat.* II. 2. 4; Sall., *Bellum Cat.* 15; Ascon., *Enarratio in Tog. Cand.* 75, 82; Plut., *Cicero* 10; and Appian, *Bella Civ.* II. 1. 2. Kaplan, *Catiline*, pp. 25–31, tried to demonstrate that not all of these rumors were true. The lascivious Clodia, sister of the firebrand *popularis* politician of this era Clodius, was immortalized in the love poems penned about her by the passionate lyric poet Catullus. For the lady and her poet, see: Edith Hamilton, *The Roman Way* (New York, 1963), pp. 75–86; Amanda Hurley, *Catullus* (London, 2004); and Aubrey Burl, *Catullus: A Poet in the Rome of Julius Caesar* (New York, 2004).

5. Ascon., *Enarratio in Tog. Cand.* 73; Appian, *Bella Civ.* II. 1. 2; Cic., *Oratio in Cat.* II. 5. 9 and *Oratio pro Caelio* 6. 13.

6. Appian, *Bella Civ.* II. 1. 2.

7. Sall., *Bellum Cat.* 18. 3 explained the situation facing Catiline in late 66: "Post paulo Catilina pecuniarum repetundarum reus prohibitus erat consulatum petere, quod intra legitumos dies profiteri nequiverat"; *cf.* Cic., *Oratio pro Caelio* 4. 10; Ascon., *Enarratio in Tog. Cand.* 75–76, 79–80; and Dio, *Hist. Rom.* XXXVI. 44. 4.

8. Sall., *Bellum Cat.* 18. 2–5; Cic., *Oratio pro Sulla* 24. 67–68 and *Oratio pro Murena* 38. 81; and Dio, *Hist. Rom.* XXXVI. 44. 3–4.

9. Cic., *Oratio in Cat.* I. 6. 16; Sall., *Bellum Cat.* 18. 4–8; Ascon., *Enarratio in Tog. Cand.* 82–83; and Dio, *Hist. Rom.* XXXVI. 44. 4.

10. The scholarship on this "First Catilinarian Conspiracy" has been both voluminous and contentious. Beesly (*Catiline*, pp. 25–26), who viewed Catiline as a proto-socialist hero, did not think that he would have participated in such an incompetent political plot; Hardy (*Catilinarian Conspiracy*, pp. 12–20), relying upon late and unreliable data in Suet., *Div. Jul.* 9, thought that the conspiracy did occur, but that Crassus and Caesar were behind it—very doubtful as both had obtained key offices for 65 and had more sensible plans for buttressing their positions against Pompey. H. Frisch, "The First Catilinarian Conspiracy: A Study in Historical Conjecture," *Classica et Mediaevalia*, vol. 9 (1947), pp. 10–36, offered a revisionist position that this supposed early plot was a fabrication of the ancient authors and did not occur; his arguments have been buttressed by R. Seager, "The First Catilinarian Conspiracy," *Historia*, vol. 13 (1964), pp. 338–47; and Ronald Syme, *Sallust* (Berkeley, 1964), pp. 86–102; and accepted by D. H. Berry, *Cicero: Political Speeches*, pp. 136, 305. On the other hand, C. E. Stevens, "The Plotting of BC 66/65," *Latomus*, vol. 22 (1963), pp. 397–435, defended the essential reliability of the ancient sources and the contemporary belief that the conspiracy had been planned; Scullard, *From the Gracchi to Nero*, pp. 105–06 and 423, also saw it as probable; while Pagán, *Conspiracy Narratives*, pp. 30 and 142, reviews the scholarship on the issue. Whether it had been planned or not, rumors about this possible conspiracy circulated in the 60s and affected attitudes toward the suspected plotters.

11. Plut., *Crassus* 6–12 and *Pompey* 6–23. For Crassus' role in putting down the gladiator revolt led by Spartacus, see Theresa Urbainczyk, *Spartacus* (London, 2004).

12. Sall., *Bellum Cat.* 19. 1–2; Ascon., *Enarratio in Tog. Cand.* 83; and Dio, *Hist. Rom.* XXXVI. 44. 5. For modern views, consult Perowne, *Death of the Republic*, pp. 160–61; and Scullard, *From the Gracchi to Nero*, p. 106. For a contrary view that Crassus was not behind the sending of Piso to Spain, see Benedict Lowe, "The Imperium of Cn. Calpurnius Piso," *Ancient Society*, vol. 34 (2004), pp. 115–25.

13. Plut., *Crassus* 13. 1; Suet., *Div. Jul.* 11; and Dio, *Hist. Rom.* XXXVII. 9. 3.

14. Sall., *Bellum Cat.* 19. 1–5; Ascon., *Enarratio in Tog. Cand.* 74; Plut., *Crassus* 13. 1; Suet., *Div. Jul.* 11; and Dio, *Hist. Rom.* XXXVI. 44. 5 and XXXVII. 9. 3. For modern accounts of Crassus in these events, see Marsh, *History of the Roman World*, pp. 162–63; Taylor, *Party Politics*, pp. 121–22; Scullard, *From the Gracchi to Nero*, pp. 106–07; and Allen Mason Ward, *Marcus Crassus and the Late Roman Republic* (London, 1977), esp. pp. 83–145.

15. Suet., *Div. Jul.* 6–11; Plut., *Caesar* 5–6, *Pompey* 25–30, and *Crassus* 13. 1; and Dio, *Hist. Rom.* XXXVI. 43. 1–2.

16. Vell., *Hist. Rom.* II. 43. 3–4; Suet., *Div. Jul.* 10–12; Plut., *Caesar* 5–6, 11. 1; Appian, *Bella Civ.* II. 1. 1; and Dio, *Hist. Rom.* XXXVII. 8. 1, 10. 1–3.

17. Suet., *Div. Jul.* 10. 2; and Plut., *Caesar* 6. 4. For modern accounts of Caesar's activities at this time, consult: Taylor, *Party Politics*, pp. 122–23; Scullard, *From the Gracchi to Nero*, pp. 107–08; Matthias Gelzer, *Caesar: Politician and Statesman* (Cambridge, MA, 1968), pp. 27–42; Michael Grant, *Julius Caesar* (New York, 1992), pp. 14–18; Millar, *The Crowd in Rome*, pp. 73–76; and Adrian Goldsworthy, *Caesar: Life of a Colossus* (New Haven, CT, 2006), pp. 96–119.

18. Cic., *Oratio pro Caelio* 6. 13; Plut., *Cicero* 10. 3; and Appian, *Bella Civ.* II. 1. 2.

19. Cic., *Oratio pro Sulla* 29. 81 and *Epistulae ad Atticum* I. 2; Ascon., *Enarratio in Tog. Cand.* 73, 76; and Appian, *Bella Civ.* II. 1. 2. Because Cicero was a native of Arpinum rather than Rome, Catiline derisively referred to him as *inquilinus*, "the lodger," a man occupying a home not his own—similar to the label "carpetbagger" in modern politics.

20. Sall., *Bellum Cat.* 17. 7; Ascon., *Enarratio in Tog. Cand.* 74, 78, 80–81; Appian, *Bella Civ.* II. 1. 2; and Dio, *Hist. Rom.* XXXVII. 10. 2–3. For modern assessments, see Marsh, *History of the Roman World*, pp. 163–64; Taylor, *Party Politics*, pp. 123–24; Kaplan, *Catiline*, pp. 48–50; and Scullard, *From the Gracchi to Nero*, pp. 106–07.

NOTES TO CHAPTER IV

1. Ancient sources providing data on the life and career of Cicero up to the beginning of his consulship in 63 include Cicero's own extant speeches given in the courts, the Senate, and the assemblies, with his election invective *Oratio in Toga Candida* preserved in Asconius' *Enarratio* particularly important for this chapter, and the beginning of his *Epistulae ad Atticum*; Sallust's *Bellum Catilinae*; Plutarch's biography on *Cicero*; and bits of information in the narratives of Velleius' *Historiae Romanae* II. 34; Appian's *Bella Civilia* II; and Dio's *Historia Romana* XXXVI and XXXVII. Among the voluminous modern biographies and studies on Cicero, old classics include H. J. Haskell, *This Was Cicero* (New York, 1942); R. E. Smith, *Cicero the Statesman* (Cambridge, 1966); F. R. Cowell, *Cicero and the Roman Republic*, 4th ed. (Baltimore, 1967); David Stockton, *Cicero: A Political Biography* (Oxford, 1971); and D. R. Shackleton Bailey, *Cicero* (New York, 1971). More recent works include Christian Habicht, *Cicero the Politician* (New Haven, 1990);

Manfred Fuhrmann, *Cicero and the Roman Republic*, tr. by W. E. Yuill (Oxford, 1992); and Anthony Everitt, *Cicero: The Life and Times of Rome's Greatest Politician* (New York, 2001).

2. Ascon., *Enarratio in Tog. Cand.* 73; Plut., *Cicero* 2–4, 7, 11. On Cicero's role as an advocate in the courts and as a writer on the law, see the recent work by Jill Harries, *Cicero and the Jurists* (London, 2006).

3. Plut., *Cicero* 3–9; Dio, *Hist. Rom.* XXXVI. 42. 1–43. 2; and Cic., *Oratio pro Roscio Amerino, Orationes in Verrem*, and *Oratio pro Lege Manilia*. For a new translation with detailed introduction and notes on the *pro Roscio Amerino*, consult D. H. Berry, *Cicero: Defense Speeches* (Oxford, 2000), pp. 3–58, 224–31; and for the same on two of the *In Verrem* speeches and the *pro Lege Manilia* (also known as *De imperio Cn. Pompei*), see Berry, *Cicero: Political Speeches*, pp. 3–133, 271–302.

4. Unlike the Tribal Assembly (used for making laws and electing lower magistrates), which had a more democratic voting system—one man, one vote within each tribal group and one vote for each of the 35 tribes into which Roman citizens were organized for making decisions in this political body—the Centuriate Assembly (primarily used for electing the upper magistrates with *imperium*) had a more hierarchical voting system: The richest citizens were placed in the upper voting classes, voted first, and had their votes weighted more heavily than those of the lower voting classes into which the rest of the Roman citizens were registered for determining elections in this political body. For modern works on this topic, consult the old classics of Léon Homo, *Roman Political Institutions from City to State*, tr. by M. R. Dobie (New York, 1962); and Lily Ross Taylor, *Roman Voting Assemblies: From the Hannibalic War to the Dictatorship of Caesar* (Ann Arbor, MI, 1966); and the more recent works of Lintott, *The Constitution of the Roman Republic*; and Millar, *The Crowd in Rome*, esp. pp.13–48.

5. Plut., *Cicero* 7; and Cic., *Oratio pro Lege Manilia, passim*. For modern comments on his early career, consult Taylor, *Party Politics*, pp. 100–118; Scullard, *From the Gracchi to Nero*, pp. 94–97; Smith, *Cicero the Statesman*, pp. 4–82; Habicht, *Cicero the Politician*, pp. 16–28; Everitt, *Cicero*, pp. 21–86; Millar, *The Crowd in Rome*, pp. 73–93; and Berry, *Cicero: Political Speeches*, pp. xiii–xvi.

6. Sall., *Bellum Cat.* 14. 1–3; and Cic., *Oratio in Cat.* II. 5. 9 for the quotations in the text; see also Cic., *Oratio pro Caelio* 5. 12; and Sall., *Bellum Cat.* 21. 2 for similar material.

7. Cic., *Ep. ad Att.* I. 1; Sall., *Bellum Cat.* 16. 4, 21. 3; Ascon., *Enarratio in Tog. Cand.* 73–74; Plut., *Cicero* 11; and Appian, *Bella Civ.* II. 1. 2.

8. Cic., *Ep. ad Att.* I. 1–2; Plut., *Cicero* 7–8; Cornelius Nepos, *De Historicis Latinis: Atticus* 1–6; and see also the electioneering pamphlet supposedly written by Cicero's brother Quintus Cicero, *Commentariolum Petitionis Consulatus ad M. Fratrem*, which offered many useful suggestions for consular campaigns during the late republican era.

9. Cic., *Ep. ad Att.* I. 1; Taylor, *Party Politics*, p. 118.

10. Ascon., *Enarratio in Tog. Cand.* 74.

11. Ascon., *Enarratio in Tog. Cand.* 73–84; Sall., *Bellum Cat.* 23. 5–24. 1; Plut., *Cicero* 10–11; and Appian, *Bella Civ.* II. 1. 2. For modern commentary on the consular election and Cicero's astute campaign therein, see Smith, *Cicero the Statesman*, pp. 92–97; Stockton, *Cicero: A Political Biography*, pp. 81–83; Habicht, *Cicero the Politician*, pp. 28–29; Everitt, *Cicero*, pp. 86–95; R. G. Lewis, *Asconius: Commentaries on Speeches of Cicero* (Oxford, 2007); and for a modern attempt to refute of many of Cicero's charges against Catiline, consult Kaplan, *Catiline*, esp. pp. 2–31, 51–56.

12. Sall., *Bellum Cat.* 24. 1–26. 1; Appian, *Bella Civ.* II. 1. 2; and Dio, *Hist. Rom.* XXXVII. 10. 4, 29. 1.
13. Cic., *Orationes de Lege Agraria* I. 1–6, II. 7–27; Plut., *Cicero* 12. 2–3; and Dio, *Hist. Rom.* XXXVII. 25. 4.
14. Cic., *Ep. ad Att.* I. 16. 6.
15. Plut., *Cicero* 12. 3–4.
16. Cicero gave four *Orationes de Lege Agraria*, of which three have survived. Ancient sources reporting on this episode include Plut., *Cicero* 12. 5; *Pompey* 39. 2; and Dio, *Hist. Rom.* XXXVII. 7, 11. 1, 25. 4. For modern comments on the machinations of Crassus and the Rullan land bill at this time and on Cicero's speeches against it, see Marsh, *History of the Roman World*, pp. 165–66; Scullard, *From the Gracchi to Nero*, p. 107; Ward, *Crassus*, pp. 152–62; Millar, *The Crowd in Rome*, pp. 101–05; and Berry, *Cicero: Political Speeches*, p. xvi, who accurately comments: "the speeches demonstrate Cicero's ability to persuade the people to vote down a proposal that was in their interest. He claimed to be a popular consul acting in the people's interest, but was actually taking a conservative line. Now that he had reached the highest place in the 'sequence of offices' (*cursus honorum*), he was always to follow the conservative, traditional, and republican line which by nature he preferred. Having been allowed to join the club, he would defend its rules to the death."
17. Plut., *Cicero* 12. 1 and 5; and Dio, *Hist. Rom.* XXXVII. 25. 3–4 and XLIV. 47. 4.
18. Sall., *Bellum Cat.* 29. 2 quoted the "last decree" and described the powers it supposedly bestowed upon the consuls. Gaius Gracchus, younger brother of Tiberius Gracchus and an early leader of the *populares* faction, was killed in 121, while Lucius Saturninus and Gaius Glaucia, popular allies and political agents of Marius, were slain in 100 under sanction of the *senatus consultum ultimum*. For these earlier events, consult Scullard, *From the Gracchi to Nero*, pp. 22–38, 46–60.
19. The few sources covering this trial are Suet., *Div. Jul.* 12; Dio, *Hist. Rom.* XXXVII. 26–28; and Cic., *Oratio pro Rabirio Perduellionis*, esp. 6. 18. For the complexity of the legal and historical issues surrounding the trial of Rabirius and the problem of the limited sources thereupon, see Millar, *The Crowd in Rome*, pp. 105–08. The *senatus consultum ultimum* was one of the important weapons Cicero would attempt to employ in defeating Catiline's revolutionary designs later in his consulship; but the legality of the "ultimate decree" was questionable throughout the late republic and has long been debated among modern scholars. On this contested issue, see Andrew Drummond, *Law, Politics and Power: Sallust and the Execution of the Catilinarian Conspirators* (Stuttgart, 1995), esp. pp. 79–95.
20. Suet., *Div. Jul.* 13; Plut., *Caesar* 7. 1–3; and Dio, *Hist. Rom.* XXXVII. 37. 1–3. For modern commentary on Caesar's actions in this period, consult Taylor, *Party Politics*, pp.122–23; Scullard, *From the Gracchi to Nero*, pp. 107–08; Gelzer, *Caesar*, pp. 42–47; Grant, *Julius Caesar*, pp. 18–20; and Goldsworthy, *Caesar*, pp. 119–26.

NOTES TO CHAPTER V

1. The ancient sources offering the most data on the final election campaign and the revolutionary conspiratorial designs of Catiline in mid and late 63 were Cicero, *Orationes in Catilinam* I and II; Sallust, *Bellum Catilinae*; Florus, *Epitomae* II. 12; Appian, *Bella Civilia* II. 1; Dio, *Historia Romana* XXXVII;

and Plutarch, *Cicero*. Modern scholarship useful on these topics again include Beesly, *Catiline*; Boissier, *La conjuration de Catilina*; Hardy, *Catilinarian Conspiracy*; Kaplan, *Catiline*; Pagán, *Conspiracy Narratives*; Smith, *Cicero the Statesman*; Stockton, *Cicero: A Political Biography*; Habicht, *Cicero the Politician*; and Everitt, *Cicero*.

2. Sall., *Bellum Cat.* 5. 6–8, 20. 8; *cf.* Florus, *Epit.* II. 12. 1. The Elizabethan Era dramatist and poet Ben Jonson (1573–1637) in his play *Catiline* (II. 165) had him reflect upon his election loss to Cicero with the words "To what a shadow I am melted!"

3. Plut., *Cicero* 10. 1 and 4; and Sall., *Bellum Cat.* 37. 10; *cf.* Appian, *Bella Civ.* II. 1. 2; and Dio, *Hist. Rom.* XXXVII. 30. 4.

4. Sall., *Bellum Cat.* 37. 1–9; Appian, *Bella Civ.* II. 1. 2; and Dio, *Hist. Rom.* XXXVII. 30. 2.

5. Cic., *Oratio in Cat.* II. 9. 20; Sall., *Bellum Cat.* 16. 4; Plut., *Cicero* 10. 3; Appian, *Bella Civ.* II. 1. 2; and Dio, *Hist. Rom.* XXXVII. 30. 4–5.

6. Sall., *Bellum Cat.* 40. 1; and Plut., *Cicero* 10. 3.

7. Sall., *Bellum Cat.* 14. 1–7, 24. 2–4; and Plut., *Cicero* 14. 1–2.

8. Cic., *Oratio pro Murena* 25. 50; and Sall., *Bellum Cat.* 17, 20–21, respectively. Sallust incorrectly placed the secret meeting and radical promises of Catiline during the campaign of 64. It may be true that Catiline had spoken of debt reduction then, but it is doubtful that he was planning a war against society, as the Sallustian quotation would indicate. These remarks more probably belong to the secret meeting, which Cicero reported in the Murena oration, i.e., to the summer of 63. For modern comments on the early dating of Sallust, consult Hardy, *Catilinarian Conspiracy*, pp. 23–30; Ronald Syme, *Sallust*, pp. 74–77; Smith, *Cicero the Statesman*, pp. 105–08; and Stockton, *Cicero: A Political Biography*, pp. 100–101.

9. Cic., *Oratio pro Murena* 7, 9, 18–19, 21 and *Ep. ad Att.* I. 1.

10. Cic., *Oratio pro Murena* 23. 46; and Dio, *Hist. Rom.* XXXVII. 29. 1.

11. Cic., *Oratio pro Murena* 23–25.

12. Cic., *Oratio pro Murena* 25. 51; Plut., *Cicero* 14. 2 and 4; and Dio, *Hist. Rom.* XXXVII. 29. 2–3.

13. Cic., *Oratio in Cat* I. 5. 11 and *Oratio pro Murena* 26. 52; Plut., *Cicero* 14. 5–6; and Dio, *Hist. Rom.* XXXVII. 29. 4–5. *Cf.* Berry, *Cicero: Political Speeches*, pp. 138–40, for some detailed modern commentary on the summer election of 63.

14. Cic., *Oratio in Cat.* I. 6. 14; Sall., *Bellum Cat.* 16. 4; and Florus, *Epit.* II. 12. 1. Ben Jonson accurately had his protagonist declare at this point (*Catiline* III. 234): "Our obiects [*sic*] must be sought with wounds, not words."

15. The fullest and most contemporary lists of the conspirators were in Cic., *Oratio in Cat.* III. 5–7; and Sall., *Bellum Cat.* 17, 43, 47. *Cf.* Florus, *Epit.* II. 12. 3; Appian, *Bella Civ.* II. 1. 2–4; Dio, *Hist. Rom.* XXXVII. 30; and Plut., *Cicero* 14–17.

16. Sall., *Bellum Cat.* 20–22; Florus, *Epit.* II. 12. 4; and Dio, *Hist. Rom.* XXXVII. 30. 3.

17. Cic., *Oratio in Cat.* I. 3. 7; Sall., *Bellum Cat.* 27. 1–2; Appian, *Bella Civ.* II. 1. 2; Dio, *Hist. Rom.* XXXVII. 30. 4–5; and Plut., *Cicero* 15. 1. For modern accounts of the conspiratorial plans of Catiline, see Beesly, *Catiline*, pp. 30–31; Boissier, *La conjuration de Catilina*, pp. 111–69; Hardy, *Catilinarian Conspiracy*, pp. 49–54; Kaplan, *Catiline*, p. 78; Smith, *Cicero the Statesman*, pp. 107–08; Stockton, *Cicero: A Political Biography*, pp. 110–14; Everitt, *Cicero*, p. 101; Scullard, *From the Gracchi to Nero*, pp. 108–09; and especially for the relationship of Catiline and Manlius, see E. J. Phillips, "Catiline's Conspiracy," *Historia*, vol. 25 (1976), pp. 441–48.

18. Sall., *Bellum Cat.* 23, 26; Florus, *Epit.* II. 12. 6; and Appian, *Bella Civ.* II. 1. 3. Sallust related that the alliance between Cicero, Fulvia, and Curius had been formed before the election of 64. Yet as Sallust was loose with chronology in a number of instances, many modern scholars think that he may have predated this alliance for dramatic effect. On this issue, consult Hardy, *Catilinarian Conspiracy,* pp. 26–29, 57–58; Syme, *Sallust,* pp. 76–81; and Pagán, *Conspiracy Narratives,* pp. 41–46.
19. Plut., *Cicero* 15. 1–2; *Crassus* 13. 2–3; and Dio, *Hist. Rom.* XXXVII. 31. 1. Hardy, in *Catilinarian Conspiracy,* pp. 54–63, hinted that Crassus himself might have written the letters "to supply the deficiencies of Cicero's intelligence department. . . ." He posited that Crassus and Caesar were trying to establish a *modus vivendi* with Pompey and that it was in their interest to assist Cicero in thwarting Catiline's schemes. But Hardy had a tendency to place Crassus and Caesar behind every important action at Rome in this decade. Ward, *Crassus,* pp. 178–84, and Stockton, *Cicero: A Political Biography,* pp. 114–15, more reasonably posited that one of Catiline's associates wrote the letters and that Crassus warned Cicero in order to distance himself from Catiline.
20. Cic., *Oratio in Cat.* I. 3. 7; Sall., *Bellum Cat.* 29 (who quotes the *senatus consultum ultimum* and its powers in full); Plut., *Cicero* 15. 3–4; and Dio, *Hist. Rom.* XXXVII. 31. 1–3. Cicero, Sallust, and Plutarch only mentioned one meeting of the Senate on the day following the delivery of the letters to the consul; but Dio posited two sessions of the Senate, one in which Cicero presented the letters and the Senate decreed an inquiry, and another during which Arrius gave his information and the Senate decreed the *senatus consultum ultimum.* The earlier sources would thus have the letters delivered to Cicero on the night of 20–21 October and one meeting of the Senate on 21 October; the later source would have the letters delivered on the night of 18–19 October and two meetings of the Senate held on 19 and 21 October. In either case, Cicero was explicit that the "ultimate decree" was passed on 21 October. For modern comments on the senatorial meeting and on the "last decree," see Hardy, *Catilinarian Conspiracy,* pp. 54–60; Kaplan, *Catiline,* pp. 78–83; and Berry, *Cicero: Political* Speeches, pp. 140–41, who favor the later evidence of two meetings. See also Stockton, *Cicero the Statesman,* p. 109; Fuhrmann, *Cicero and the Roman Republic,* p. 68; and Everitt, *Cicero,* pp. 101–02, who favor the earlier evidence of one senatorial meeting; and Drummond, *Law, Politics and Power,* pp. 79–95, who analyzes the *senatus consultum ultimum.*
21. Cic., *Oratio in Cat.* I. 3. 7; Plut., *Cicero* 16. 1; Florus, *Epit.* I. 42; Appian, *Bella Civ.* II. 1. 3; and Dio, *Hist. Rom.* XXXVII. 31. 3.
22. Sall., *Bellum Cat.* 30. 1–7; and Dio, *Hist. Rom.* XXXVII. 31. 3.
23. Cic., *Oratio in Cat.* I. 8. 19; Sall., *Bellum Cat.* 31. 4; and Dio, *Hist. Rom.* XXXVII. 32. 1–3. *Cf.* Hardy, *Catilinarian Conspiracy,* pp. 63–64; and Stockton, *Cicero: A Political Biography,* pp. 116–17: *de vi* was an indictment against someone who was accused of employing force to overthrow the government.
24. Cic., *Oratio in Cat.* I. 3. 8.
25. Cic., *Oratio in Cat.* I. 4 and *Oratio pro Sulla* 5, 6, 18, 19; Sall., *Bellum Cat.* 27. 3–28. 1; Florus, *Epit.* II. 12; Appian, *Bella Civ.* II. 3; Dio, *Hist. Rom.* XXXVII. 32. 3–4; and Plut., *Cicero* 16. 2. For the modern debate that Sallust may have antedated this meeting to earlier in October, consult Hardy, *Catilinarian Conspiracy,* pp. 51–65; Syme, *Sallust,* pp. 77–84; and Stockton, *Cicero: A Political Biography,* p. 117.

NOTES TO CHAPTER VI

1. Ancient sources most useful for Cicero's victory over Catiline and his urban and rural followers in late 63 and early 62 were Cicero's own *Orationes in Catilinam* I–IV; Sallust's *Bellum Catilinae*; Florus' *Epitomae* II. 12; Appian's *Bella Civilia* II. 1; Dio's *Historia Romana* XXXVII. 32–42; and Plutarch's *Cicero* and *Cato the Younger*. Modern works useful for this period again include Beesly, *Catiline*; Boissier, *La conjuration de Catilina*; Hardy, *Catilinarian Conspiracy*; Kaplan, *Catiline*; Pagán, *Conspiracy Narratives*; Smith, *Cicero the Statesman*; Stockton, *Cicero: A Political Biography*; Everitt, *Cicero*; Drummond, *Law, Politics and Power*; Berry, *Cicero: Political Speeches*; and Millar, *The Crowd in Rome*.
2. Cic., *Oratio in Cat.* I. 4. 10 and *Oratio pro Sulla* 6. 18; Sall., *Bellum Cat.* 28 1–3; Dio, *Hist. Rom.* XXXVII. 32. 4–33. 1; and Plut., *Cicero* 16. 2. On the *salutatio* custom, see Alfred J. Church, *Roman Life in the Days of Cicero* (New York, 1883), pp. 134–35.
3. The language employed by Cicero in *Oratio in Cat.* I. 1. 1 (*superiore nocte* = "on the night before") and in I. 4. 1 (*noctem illam superiorem* = "that earlier night") indicated that there was an intervening day and night between the nocturnal conspiratorial meeting at the house of Laeca on 6–7 November and the diurnal senatorial meeting in the temple of Jupiter on 8 November. The Loeb and Penguin editions of the *Orations Against Catiline* render these Latin phrases fairly literally as "the night before last"; D. H. Berry, unwisely following fallacious reasoning about the dating of the events of this period, renders them incorrectly as "yesterday evening" in the Oxford World's Classics editions of the orations in *Cicero: Political Speeches*, pp. 157, 159 (with introductory material and notes on this issue on pp. 142, 302–03); as with most modern scholars, I have followed herein the more literal translations and traditional dates.
4. Cic., *Oratio in Cat.* I (with specific references to or from 1. 1–2, 7. 16, and 13. 33); Sall., *Bellum Cat.* 21. 6; and Plut., *Cicero* 16. 3. Stockton, in *Cicero: A Political Biography*, pp. 117–18, accurately commented that "As rhetoric it is magnificent and overwhelming. The great drum-roll of his oratory beats on the ear." For a new translation with detailed introduction and notes on the *First Catilinarian*, consult Berry, *Cicero: Political Speeches*, pp. 134–69, 302–06.
5. Sall., *Bellum Cat.* 31. 7–32. 1, 37; and Plut., *Cicero* 16. 4.
6. Sall., *Bellum Cat.* 32. 2, 34. 2–35. 6; Plut., *Cicero* 16. 4; Florus, *Epit.* II. 12. 1. 7–8; Appian, *Bella Civ.* II. 3; and Dio, *Hist. Rom.* XXXVII. 33. 2.
7. Cic., *Oratio in Cat.* II. For a new translation with detailed introduction and notes on the *Second Catilinarian* (but incorrectly dated to 8 November), see Berry, *Cicero: Political Speeches*, pp. 134–56, 170–80, 306–08; and also consult Millar, *The Crowd in Rome*, p. 109, for the purpose of such *contio* meetings in the Forum and this speech of Cicero to influence the common people and bring them to his side against Catiline and the conspirators..
8. Cic., *Oratio in Cat.* II. 4. 6; Sall., *Bellum Cat.* 36. 1; Plut., *Cicero* 16. 4; and Dio, *Hist. Rom.* XXXVII. 33. 2. The *fasces* were bundles of sticks around an axe. They represented the magistrate's authority and right of command—his *imperium*. As a praetor, Catiline had held the *imperium* a few years earlier; but his assumption of the *fasces* and *imperium* in late 63 was an illegal and revolutionary act.
9. Sall., *Bellum Cat.* 36. 2–3, 39. 5; and Dio, *Hist. Rom.* XXXVII. 33. 2–4, 36. 4.
10. Cic., *Oratio pro Murena*; and Plut., *Cato the Younger* 21. For an appreciation of the entertainment value of this court speech of Cicero in poking fun at the

legal silliness of Silanus and at the Stoic stiffness of Cato (with the latter even sourly observing "What a comic we have for a consul"), consult Everitt, *Cicero*, pp. 105–06; and for a new translation with detailed introduction and notes on the *pro Murena*, see Berry, *Cicero: Defense Speeches*, pp. 59–106, 232–46.

11. Cic., *Oratio in Cat.* III. 4. 9; Sall., *Bellum Cat.* 39. 6; and Plut., *Cicero* 16. 4–17. 4.

12. Cic., *Oratio in Cat.* III. 4. 10 and *Oratio in Cat.* IV. 6. 13; Sall., *Bellum Cat.* 39. 6; Plut., *Cicero* 18. 1–2; Florus, *Epit.* II. 12. 8; Appian, *Bella Civ.* II. 1. 3–4; and Dio, *Hist. Rom.* XXXVII. 34. 1.

13. Cic., *Oratio in Cat.* III. 1. 3–2. 4; Sall., *Bellum Cat.* 40. 1–41. 5; Plut., *Cicero* 18. 3; Florus, *Epit.* II. 12. 9; Appian, *Bella Civ.* II. 1. 4; and Dio, *Hist. Rom.* XXXVII. 34. 1. On the Allobroges and Vienne, consult Paul MacKendrick, *Roman France* (London, 1971), pp. 81–83.

14. Cic., *Oratio in Cat.* III. 2. 4, 4. 9; Sall., *Bellum Cat.* 41. 5, 43. 2, 44. 1–6, Plut., *Cicero* 18. 3–4; and Appian, *Bella Civ.* II. 1. 4.

15. Cic., *Oratio in Cat.* III. 2. 5–3. 6 and *Oratio pro Flacco* 40. 102; Sall., *Bellum Cat.* 45; Plut., *Cicero* 18. 5. For modern accounts of the capture of documentary evidence against the conspirators, see Hardy, *Catilinarian Conspiracy*, pp. 73–77; Kaplan, *Catiline*, pp. 94–98; Stockton, *Cicero: A Political Biography*, pp. 126–28; Everitt, *Cicero*, p. 106; and Shane Butler, *The Hand of Cicero* (London, 2002), pp. 85–86.

16. Cic., *Oratio in Cat.* III. 3–6; Sall., *Bellum Cat.* 47. 1–48. 2; Plut., *Cicero* 19. 1–2; Florus, *Epit.* II. 12. 9; Appian, *Bella Civ.* II. 1. 4–5; and Dio, *Hist. Rom.* XXXVII. 34. 2. On the importance of documentary evidence in proving the guilt of the conspirators, consult Butler, *The Hand of Cicero*, pp. 85–102. It should also be noted that Crassus and Caesar each received one of the guilty criminals, and this should indicate that they were no longer associated with the plots of Catiline. On this and the meeting of 3 December, see Marsh, *History of the Roman World*, pp. 167–68; Ward, *Crassus*, pp. 188–89; Gelzer, *Caesar*, p. 49; Stockton, *Cicero: A Political Biography*, pp. 128–30; and D. A. March, "Cicero and the Gang of Five," *Classical World*, vol. 82 (1988–89), pp. 225–34.

17. Cic., *Oratio in Cat.* III; and Sall., *Bellum Cat.* 48. 1–2. For a new translation with detailed introduction and notes on the *Third Catilinarian*, consult Berry, *Cicero: Political Speeches*, pp. 134–56, 181–92, 308–13; and for its effectiveness in changing the sentiments of the urban populace, see Millar, *The Crowd in Rome*, pp. 109–10.

18. Plut., *Cicero* 19. 3–20. 2; and Dio, *Hist. Rom.* XXXVII. 35. 4. Smith, *Cicero the Statesman*, p. 117; Everitt, *Cicero*, p. 107; and most recently Susan Treggiari, *Terentia, Tullia and Publilia: The Woman of Cicero's Family* (London, 2007), pp. 44–47, have included the *Bona Dea* incident in their accounts of this dangerous time; but as the story was only recorded in the later writings of Plutarch and Dio, many other scholars have left it out of their narratives. Whether this incident did or did not actually occur cannot thus be determined with certainty. However, as Plutarch was a priest at the sacred site of Delphi and very interested in spiritual phenomena, he would have been the one ancient author writing about these events most interested in recording such a religious portent.

19. Sall., *Bellum Cat.* 48. 3–50. 1; Plut., *Crassus* 13. 2–3 and *Caesar* 7. 3–8. 2; Suet., *Div. Jul.* 14; Cic., *Oratio in Cat.* IV. 3. 5; and Dio, *Hist. Rom.* XXX-VII. 35. 1–2.

20. Cic., *Oratio in Cat.* IV. 8. 17 and *Ep. ad Att.* XII. 21. 1; Sall., *Bellum Cat.* 50. 1–3; Appian, *Bella Civ.* II. 1. 5; and Dio, *Hist. Rom.* XXXVII. 35. 3.

21. The senatorial meeting of 5 December 63 was one of the best-recorded incidents in Cicero's consulship and of Catiline's conspiracy with Cicero's *Oratio*

in Catilinam IV published only a few years after it was given, and Sallust's *Bellum Catilinae* 50. 3–55. 1 reporting the session and the speeches of Caesar and Cato in full within twenty years after the event (though it is doubtful that we have the exact wording of those speeches as originally given). *Cf.* Vell., *Hist. Rom.* II. 35. 1–4; Florus, *Epit.* II. 12. 10–11; Appian, *Bella Civ.* II. 1. 5–6; Dio, *Hist. Rom.* XXXVII. 36. 1–3; Suet., *Div. Jul.* 14; Plut., *Cicero* 20. 3–21. 4, *Caesar* 7. 4–8. 2, and *Cato the Younger* 22–23. For a new translation with detailed introduction and notes on the *Fourth Catilinarian* of Cicero, see Berry, *Cicero: Political Speeches*, pp. 134–56, 193–203, 313–17; and for comment on Sallust's treatment of the speeches of Caesar and Cato, consult Syme, *Sallust*, esp. pp. 73, 108–20. For modern commentary on this meeting and its decision, see Bossier, *La conjuration de Catilina*, pp. 215–59; Hardy, *Catilinarian Conspiracy*, pp. 85–97; Kaplan, *Catiline*, pp. 104–16; Smith, *Cicero the Statesman*, pp. 119–24; Stockton, *Cicero: A Political Biography*, pp. 133–40; and Everitt, *Cicero*, pp. 108–11; and for the most detailed account of the legal problems involved in Cicero's decision to put the conspirators to death, consult Drummond, *Law, Politics and Power: Sallust and the Execution of the Catilinarian Conspirators*, pp. 21–113.

22. Sall., *Bellum Cat.* 55; Vell., *Hist. Rom.* II. 34. 4, 35. 5; Florus, *Epit.* II. 12. 11; Appian, *Bella Civ.* II. 1. 6; and Plut., *Cicero* 22. 1–4. Millar, *The Crowd in Rome*, pp. 110–12, deals with the dramatic effect that the executions must have had upon the people and the approval of the mob for Cicero's action. The *Tullianum* had gotten its name either from a spring in the area (*tullius*) or, as the Roman people thought, from one of their kings who had supposedly built the prison in the sixth century (Servius Tullius). Although Cicero was hailed as a hero under the immediate danger of the conspiracy, his illegal action of putting citizens to death without the official decision of a Roman court (which a decree of the Senate was not) would come back to haunt him a few years later. For the modern debate on the executions, see the references in the previous note.

23. Sall., *Bellum Cat.* 42; Appian, *Bella Civ.* II. 1. 7; and Dio, *Hist. Rom.* XXXVII. 36. 3–4.

24. Sall., *Bellum Cat.* 56–61; Vell., *Hist. Rom.* II. 35. 5; Florus, *Epit.* II. 12. 12; Appian, *Bella Civ.* II. 1. 7; and Dio, *Hist. Rom.* XXXVII. 39. 1–41. 4.

25. Plut., *Cicero* 23. 1–3; and Appian, *Bellum Civ.* II. 1. 7.

NOTES TO CHAPTER VII

1. Ancient narrative histories covering the later phases of the "Roman Revolution" from 62 to 31 BC summarized here were Velleius' *Historiae Romanae* II. 36–89; Florus' *Epitomae* II. 13–21; Appian's *Bella Civilia* II. 2–V. 145; and Dio's *Historia Romana* XXXVII. 43–LII. 42; with the *Epistulae* and philosophical works of Cicero; the military *Commentarii* of Caesar; Suetonius' biographies of *Divus Julius* and *Divus Augustus*; and Plutarch's biographies of *Crassus, Pompey, Cicero, Caesar, Cato the Younger,* and *Antony* adding many colorful details. Modern studies covering this period include: Ronald Syme, *The Roman Revolution* (Oxford, 1939); H. H. Scullard, *From the Gracchi to Nero: A History of Rome from 133 BC to AD 68*, 5th ed. (London, 1982); Allen Mason Ward, *Marcus Crassus and the Late Roman Republic* (Colombia, MO, 1977); Peter Greenhalgh, *Pompey: The Republican Prince* (Columbia, MO, 1982); R. J. Seager, *Pompey the Great: A Political Biography*, 2nd ed. (Oxford, 2002); Matthias Gelzer, *Caesar: Politician and Statesman* (Cambridge, MA, 1968); Adrian Goldsworthy, *Caesar: Life*

of a Colossus (New Haven, CT, 2006); Christian Habicht, *Cicero the Politician* (Baltimore, MD, 1990); Anthony Everitt, *Cicero: The Life and Times of Rome's Greatest Politician* (New York, 2001); W. W. Tarn and M. P. Charlesworth, *Octavian, Antony and Cleopatra* (Cambridge, 1965); Eleanor Goltz Huzar, *Mark Antony: A Biography* (Minneapolis, MN, 1978); A. H. M. Jones, *Augustus* (New York, 1970); Pat Southern, *Augustus* (London, 1998); and Anthony Everitt, *Augustus: The Life of Rome's First Emperor* (New York, 2006).

2. The perceptive comments of Thucydides and Sallust on human political behavior in the stress of chaotic revolutionary eras are found in *The Peloponnesian War* III. 82–83 and *The War of Catiline* 38. 3, respectively. The final quotations at the end of the text are from Sall., *Bellum Iug.* 42. 4; and Cic., *De Officiis* I. 22. 77. Weekly news magazines, daily newspapers, the twenty-four-hour cable television news channels, and Internet blogs clearly exhibit the divisive trends in modern politics mirroring those of ancient times.

Bibliography

ANCIENT SOURCES*

Appian. *Bella Civilia* = *Civil Wars*. Greek text and English translation by H. White in the Loeb Classical Library. Cambridge, MA: Harvard University Press, 1958.

———. *The Civil Wars*. Eng. tr. by John Carter in the Penguin Classics. London: Penguin, 1996.

Asconius (Quintus Asconius Pedianus). *Enarratio ad Orationem in Toga Candida* = *A Commentary on the Oration in the White Toga*. La. text ed. by A. C. Clark in *Orationem Ciceronis Quinque Enarratio*. Oxford: Clarendon Press, 1907.

———. *Commentaries on the Speeches of Cicero*. Eng. tr. and commentary by R. G. Lewis. New York: Oxford University Press, 2007.

Cicero (Marcus Tullius Cicero). *Epistulae ad Atticum* = *Letters to Atticus*. La. texts and Eng. tr. by D. R. Shackleton Bailey in the LCL. 3 Vols. Cambridge, MA: Harvard University Press, 1999.

———. *Libri III de Officiis* = *Three Books on Duties*. La. text and Eng. tr. by W. Miller in the LCL. Cambridge, MA: Harvard University Press, 1913.

———. *Libri VI de Re Publica* = *Six Books on the Republic*. La. text and Eng. tr. by C. W. Keyes in the LCL. Cambridge, MA: Harvard University Press, 1928.

———. *Oratio pro Caelio* = *Oration for Caelius*. La. text and Eng. tr. by R. Gardner in the LCL. Cambridge, MA: Harvard University Press, 1958.

———. *Orationes in Catilinam I—IV* = *Orations against Catiline I–IV*. La. texts and Eng. tr. by C. MacDonald in the LCL. Cambridge, MA: Harvard University Press, 1977.

———. *Catilinarians*. La. texts and commentary by Andrew R. Dyke. Cambridge: Cambridge University Press, 2008.

———. *Oratio pro Flacco* = *Oration for Flaccus*. La. text and Eng. tr. by C. MacDonald in the LCL. Cambridge, MA: Harvard University Press, 1967.

———. *Orationes de Lege Agraria contra Rullum I–III* = *Orations concerning the Agrarian Law against Rullus I–III*. La. texts and Eng. tr. by J. H. Freese in the LCL. Cambridge, MA: Harvard University Press, 1930.

———. *Oratio pro Lege Manilia* = *Oration for the Manilian Law*. La. text and Eng. tr. by H. G. Hodge in the LCL. Cambridge, MA: Harvard University Press, 1928.

———. *Oratio pro Murena* = *Oration for Murena*. La. text and Eng. tr. by C. MacDonald in the LCL. Cambridge, MA: Harvard University Press, 1977.

———. *Oratio pro Rabirio Perduellionis* = *Oration for Rabirius on Treason*. La. text and Eng. tr. by H. G. Hodge in the LCL. Cambridge, MA: Harvard University Press, 1928.

————. *Oratio pro Sestio* = *Oration for Sestius*. La. text and Eng. tr. by R. Gardner in the LCL. Cambridge, MA: Harvard University Press, 1958.

————. *Oratio pro Sulla* = *Oration for Sulla*. La. text and Eng. tr. by C. MacDonald in the LCL. Cambridge, MA: Harvard University Press, 1967.

————. *Orationes in Verrem* = *Orations against Verres*. La. text and Eng. tr. by L. H. G. Greenwood in the LCL. 2 Vols. Cambridge, MA: Harvard University Press, 1928/1935.

————. *Defense Speeches*. Eng. tr. and notes by D. H. Berry in Oxford World's Classics. Oxford: Oxford University Press, 2001.

————. *Political Speeches*. Eng. tr. and notes by D. H. Berry in Oxford World's Classics. Oxford: Oxford University Press, 2006.

————. *Selected Political Speeches*. Eng. tr. by M. Grant in the Penguin Classics. London: Penguin, 1969.

————. *Selected Works*. Eng. tr. by M. Grant in the Penguin Classics. London: Penguin, 1960.

Cicero (Quintus Tullius Cicero). *Commentariolum Petitionis Consulatus ad M. Fratrum* = *Commentary on Running for the Consulship to Brother Marcus*. La. text ed. by L. C. Purser in Oxford Classical Texts. Oxford: Oxford University Press, 1902.

————. *Commentariolum Petitionis*. La. text and Eng. tr. by D. R. Shackleton Bailey in the LCL. Cambridge, MA: Harvard University Press, 2002.

Dio (Cassius Dio Cocceianus). *Historia Romana* = *Roman History*. Gk. text and Eng. tr. by E. Cary and H. Foster in the LCL. 9 vols. Cambridge, MA: Harvard University Press, 1914.

Florus (Lucius Annius Florus). *Epitomae de Tito Livio Bellorum Omnium Annorum DCC* = *an Epitome of All the Wars of Seven Hundred Years from Titus Livius*. La. text and Eng. tr. by E. S. Forster in the LCL. Cambridge, MA: Harvard University Press, 1929.

Plutarch. *Bioi* = *Parallel Lives of the Noble Greeks and Romans* (*Tiberius Gracchus, Gaius Gracchus, Gaius Marius, Sulla, Crassus, Pompey, Cicero, Cato the Younger, Caesar, Antony*). Gk. texts and Eng. tr. by Bernadotte Perrin in the LCL. 11 Vols. Cambridge, MA: Harvard University Press, 1916–1921.

————. *Fall of the Roman Republic: Six Lives by Plutarch*. Eng. tr. by R. Warner in the Penguin Classics. London: Penguin, 1958; Revised ed. by R. Seager, 2005.

Sallust (Gaius Sallustius Crispus). *Bellum Catilinae* = *The War of Catiline* and *Bellum Iugurthinum* = *The Jugurthine War*. La. texts and Eng. tr. by J. C. Rolfe in the LCL. Cambridge, MA: Harvard University Press, 1921.

————. *Bellum Catilinae*. La. text and commentary by J. T. Ramsey. 2007. Reprinted with corrections and amendments, Oxford: Oxford University Press, 2009.

————. *The Jugurthine War, The Conspiracy of Catiline*. Eng. tr. by S. A. Hanford in the Penguin Classics. London: Penguin, 1963.

————. *Catiline's War, The Jugurthine War, Histories*. Eng. tr. by A. J. Woodman in the Penguin Classics. London: Penguin, 2008.

Suetonius (Gaius Suetonius Tranquillus). *De Vita Caesarum* = *On the Life of the Caesars* (*Divus Julius, Divus Augustus*). La. texts and Eng. tr. by J. C. Rolfe in the LCL. Cambridge, MA: Harvard University Press, 1914.

————. *The Twelve Caesars*. Eng. tr. by R. Graves in the Penguin Classics. 1957. Revised ed. by M. Grant, 1979 and by James Rives in 2007, London: Penguin.

————. *Lives of the Caesars*. Eng. tr. by C. Edwards in Oxford World's Classics. Oxford: Oxford University Press, 2001.

Velleius (Velleius Paterculus). *Libri Duo Historiae Romanae* = *Two Books of Roman History*. La. text and Eng. tr. by F. W. Shipley in the LCL. Cambridge, MA: Harvard University Press, 1924.

*These are the most important ancient sources for the Ciceronian Era and the Catilinarian Conspiracy. Where available, the Loeb Classical Library editions (which contain the Greek or Latin texts with facing pages of English translations) and the Penguin Classics and Oxford World's Classics editions (which provide useful English translations) have been listed above. Many of these are also available in other Latin or Greek editions, such as the Oxford Classical Texts and the Cambridge Commentaries.

MODERN SCHOLARSHIP*

Alexander, M. C. *Trials in the Late Roman Republic: 149 BC to 50 BC.* Phoenix, Suppl. 26, Toronto, 1990.

Batstone, W. "Cicero's Construction of Consular *Ethos* in the *First Catilinarian.*" *Transactions of the American Philological Association*, vol. 24 (1994), pp. 211–66.

Berry, D. H. "*Equester Ordo Tuus Est:* Did Cicero Win his Cases because of his Support for the *Equites?*" *Classical Quarterly*, n.s., vol. 53 (2003), pp. 222–34.

Beesly, Edward Spencer. *Catiline, Clodius, and Tiberius.* London: Chapman and Hall, 1878.

Bispham, Edward. *The Roman Republic: 264–44 BC.* London: Routledge, 2009.

Boissier, Gaston. *La conjuration de Catilina.* Paris: Libriarie Hachette, 1905.

Boatwright, Mary T., Gargola, Daniel J., and Talbert, Richard J. A. *The Romans: From Village to Empire.* Oxford: Oxford University Press, 2004.

Bringmann, K. "Sallusts Umgang mit der historischen Wahrheit in seiner Darstellung der catilinarischen Verschwörung." *Philologus*, vol. 116 (1972), pp. 98–113.

Brunt, P. A. "The Conspiracy of Catiline." *History Today*, vol. 13 (January, 1963), pp. 14–21.

———. "The *Equites* in the Late Republic." *Second International Conference of Economic History*, 1962 (Paris, 1965), vol. I, pp. 117–37.

———. *The Fall of the Roman Republic and Related Essays.* Oxford: Clarendon Press, 1988.

———. "Patronage and Politics in the Verrines." *Chiron*, vol. 10 (1989), pp. 272–89.

———. "The Roman Mob." *Past and Present*, vol. 35 (1966), pp. 3–27.

Burl, Aubrey. *Catullus: A Poet in the Rome of Julius Caesar.* New York: Carroll & Graf, 2004.

Butcher, Kevin. *Roman Syria and the Near East.* London: The British Museum Press, 2003.

Butler, Shane. *The Hand of Cicero.* London: Routledge, 2002.

Cape, R. W. "The Rhetoric of Politics in Cicero's *Fourth Catilinarian.*" *American Journal of Philology*, vol. 116 (1995), pp. 255–77.

Church, Alfred J. *Roman Life in the Days of Cicero.* New York: Dodd, Mead and Company, 1883.

Cowell, F. R. *Cicero and the Roman Republic.* Baltimore, MD: Penguin, 1967.

———. *Life in Ancient Rome.* New York: G. P. Putman's Sons, 1961.

Drexler, H. *Die catilinarische Verschwörung: Ein Quellenheft.* Darmstadt, 1976.

Drummond, Andrew. *Law, Politics and Power: Sallust and the Execution of the Catilinarian Conspirators.* Stuttgart: Franz Steiner Verlag, 1995.

Earl, D. *The Political Thought of Sallust.* Cambridge: Cambridge University Press, 1961.

Evans, Richard. *Gaius Marius: A Political Biography.* Pretoria: University of South Africa, 1994.

Everitt, Anthony. *Augustus: The Life of Rome's First Emperor.* New York: Random House, 2006.

———. *Cicero: The Life and Times of Rome's Greatest Politician.* New York: Random House, 2001.

Frazel, T. D. "The Composition and Circulation of Cicero's *In Verrem.*" *Classical Quarterly,* n.s., vol. 54 (2004), pp. 128–42.

Frisch, H. "The First Catilinarian Conspiracy: A Study in Historical Conjecture." *Classica et Mediaevalia,* vol. 9 (1947), pp. 10–36.

Fuhrmann, Manfred. *Cicero and the Roman Republic.* Tr. by W. E. Yuill. Oxford: Blackwell, 1992.

Gelzer, Matthias. *Caesar: Politician and Statesman.* Tr. by Peter Needham. Cambridge: MA: Harvard University Press, 1968.

Goldsworthy, Adrian. *Caesar: Life of a Colossus.* New Haven, CT: Yale University Press, 2006.

Grant, Michael. *Julius Caesar.* New York: M. Evans & Company, 1992.

Greenhalgh, Peter. *Pompey: The Republican Prince.* Columbia, MO: University of Missouri Press, 1982.

———. *Pompey: The Roman Alexander.* Columbia, MO: University of Missouri Press, 1981.

Gruen, Erich S. *The Last Generation of the Roman Republic.* Berkeley, CA: University of California Press, 1974.

Habicht, Christian. *Cicero the Politician.* Baltimore, MD: Johns Hopkins University Press, 1990.

Hamilton, Edith. *The Roman Way to Western Civilization.* New York: The New American Library, 1957.

Hardy, E. G. *The Catilinarian Conspiracy in Its Context: A Re-Study of the Evidence.* Oxford: Basil Blackwell, 1924.

Harries, Jill. *Cicero and the Jurists.* London: Duckworth, 2006.

Haskell, H. J. *This Was Cicero.* Greenwich, CT: Fawcett Publications, 1942.

Holland, Tom. *Rubicon: The Last Years of the Roman Republic.* New York: Doubleday, 2003.

Homo, Léon. *Roman Political Institutions from City to State.* New York: Barnes & Noble, 1966.

Hurley, Amanda. *Catullus.* London: Bristol Classical Press, 2004.

Huzar, Eleanor Goltz. *Mark Antony: A Biography.* Minneapolis, MN: University of Minnesota Press, 1978.

Jones, A. H. M. *Augustus.* New York: W. W. Norton & Company, 1970.

———. *The Criminal Courts of the Roman Republic and Principate.* Oxford: Oxford University Press, 1972.

Jonson, Ben. *Catiline.* Ed. by C. H. Herford and Percy Simpson. Oxford: Clarendon Press, 1937.

Kaplan, Arthur. *Catiline: The Man and His Role in the Roman Revolution.* New York: Exposition Press, 1968.

Keaveney, Arthur. *Sulla: The Last Republican.* 2nd ed. London: Routledge, 2005.

———. *Lucullus: A Life.* London: Routledge, 1992.

Last, H. "Sallust and Caesar in the *Bellum Catilinae.*" *Mélanges de philologie, de littérature et d'histoire ancienne offerts à J. Marouzeau,* 1948, pp. 355–69.

Leach, John. *Pompey the Great.* London: Croom Helm, 1978.

Lintott, Andrew. *The Constitution of the Roman Republic.* Oxford: Oxford University Press, 1999.

———. *Urban Violence in Republican Rome.* 2nd ed. Oxford: Oxford University Press, 1995.

Lowe, Benedict. "The Imperium of Cn. Calpurnius Piso." *Ancient Society*, vol. 34 (2004), pp. 115–25.

March, D. A. "Cicero and the 'Gang of Five.'" *Classical World*, vol. 82 (1988–89), pp. 225–34.

Marsh, Frank Burr. *A History of the Roman World from 146 to 30 BC*. 3rd ed. New York: Methuen & Company, 1962.

MacKendrick, Paul. *Roman France*. London: G. Bell & Sons, 1971.

McIlwain, Charles Howard. *Constitutionalism: Ancient & Modern*. Ithaca, NY: Cornell University Press, 1947.

Millar, Fergus. *The Crowd in Rome in the Late Republic*. Ann Arbor: University of Michigan Press, 1998.

Mommsen, Theodor. *The History of Rome*. A New Edition by Dero A. Saunders and John H. Collins. Cleveland: The World Publishing Company, 1958.

Münzer, F. *Römische Adelsparteien und Adelsfamilien*. Stuttgart: J. B. Metzlersche Verlagsbuchhandlung, 1920.

Odahl, Charles Matson. *The Catilinarian Conspiracy*. New Haven, CT: College & University Press, 1971.

———. "Faesulae: Roman Remains Above Florence." *The Quest*, vol. 4, 2 (1972), pp. 2, 4, 6.

Parenti, Michael. *The Assassination of Julius Caesar*. New York: The New Press, 2003.

Perowne, Stewart. *Death of the Roman Republic from 146 BC to the Birth of the Roman Empire*. New York: Doubleday & Company, 1968.

Phillips, E. J. "Catiline's Conspiracy." *Historia*, vol. 25 (1976), pp. 441–48.

Pöhlmann, R. von. *Geschichte der sozialen Frage und des Sozialismus in der antiken Welt*. 3rd ed. Munich: Beck, 1925.

Potter, David. *Ancient Rome: A New History*. London: Thames & Hudson, 2009.

Powell, Jonathan, and Peterson, Jeremy. *Cicero the Advocate*. Oxford: Oxford University Press, 2004.

Sandys, John Edwin, Ed. *A Companion to Latin Studies*. 3rd ed. New York: Hafner Publishing Company, 1963.

Scullard, H. H. *From the Gracchi to Nero: A History of Rome from 133 BC to AD 68*. 5th ed. London: Routledge, 1982.

Seager, R. J. *Pompey the Great: A Political Biography*. 2nd ed. Oxford: Oxford University Press, 2002.

Shackleton Bailey, D. R. *Cicero*. New York: Charles Scribner's Sons, 1971.

Shotter, David. *The Fall of the Roman Republic*. 2nd ed. London: Routledge, 2005.

Smith, R. E. *Cicero the Statesman*. Cambridge: Cambridge University Press, 1966.

———. *The Failure of the Roman Republic*. Cambridge: Cambridge University Press, 1955.

Southern, Pat. *Augustus*. London: Routledge, 1998.

Stevens, C. E. "The Plotting of BC 66/65." *Latomus*, vol. 22 (1963), pp. 397–435.

Stockton, David. *Cicero: A Political Biography*. Oxford: Oxford University Press, 1971.

Syme, Ronald. *The Roman Revolution*. Oxford: Oxford University Press, 1939.

———. *Sallust*. Berkeley, CA: University of California Press, 1964.

Tarn, W. W., and Charlesworth, M. P. *Octavian, Antony and Cleopatra*. Cambridge: Cambridge University Press, 1965.

Taylor, Lily Ross. *Party Politics in the Age of Caesar*. Berkeley, CA: University of California Press, 1964.

———. *Roman Voting Assemblies: From the Hannibalic War to the Dictatorship of Caesar*. Ann Arbor, MI: University of Michigan Press, 1966.

Treggiari, Susan. *Terentia, Tullia and Publilia: The Women of Cicero's Family*. London: Routledge, 2007.

Urbainczyk, Theresa. *Spartacus*. London: Bristol Classical Press, 2004.

Ward, Allen Mason. *Marcus Crassus and the Late Roman Republic*. Columbia, MO: University of Missouri Press, 1977.

Warner, Rex. *The Young Caesar*. New York: The New American Library, 1963.

Waters, K. H. "Cicero, Sallust, and Catiline." *Historia*, vol. 19 (1970), pp. 195–215.

Williams, Richard S. "The Appointment of Glabrio (cos. 67) to the Eastern Command."*Phoenix*, vol. 38 (1984), pp. 221–34.

Williams, Richard S. "The Role of *Amicitia* in the Career of A. Gabinius (Cos. 58)." *Phoenix*, vol. 32 (1978), pp. 195–210.

Yavetz, Z. "The Failure of Catiline's Conspiracy." *Historia*, vol. 12 (1963), pp. 485–99.

*Scholarship on the late Roman Republic in general, and on Cicero and Catiline in particular, is legion, and no bibliography thereupon can be complete. The above listed works, however, provide comprehensive coverage of the major subjects and prominent people in the era, and offer curious readers the opportunity to access both old classics and new scholarship in the field.

Index